A LASTING IMPRESSION

The Art and Life of Regina Dorland Robinson

A LASTING IMPRESSION

The Art and Life of
Regina Dorland Robinson

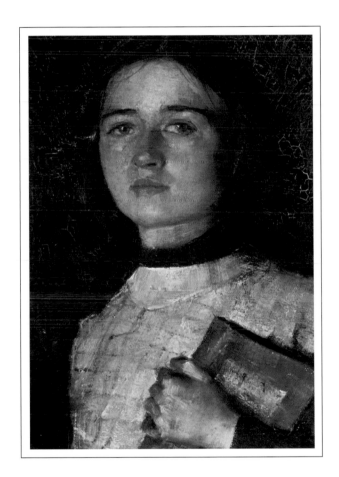

BY DAWNA CURLER

with research assistance by Sue Waldron

FOR THE SOUTHERN OREGON HISTORICAL SOCIETY

A Lasting Impression:
The Art and Life of Regina Dorland Robinson
by Dawna Curler

Publisher:
Southern Oregon Historical Society
Jacksonville, Oregon

Editors: John Enders, Harley Patrick, Southern Oregon Historical Society
Cover and Book Design: Chris Molé Design, Ashland, Oregon

Printed and bound in China by
C & C Offset Printing Co., Ltd.
A Lasting Impression: The Art and Life of Regina Dorland Robinson / Dawna Curler
ISBN: 978-0-9793894-0-5
First edition 10 9 8 7 6 5 4 3 2 1

ACKNOWLEDGMENTS

Sue Waldron, a former staff researcher for the Southern Oregon Historical Society, played a vital role in the development of this book. She began investigating Dorland Robinson's story in 1992 as the Southern Oregon Historical Society prepared an exhibit of Dorland's artwork. Sue's article, "A Brief Bloom," published by the Society in the 1992 summer edition of *The Table Rock Sentinel* was, until now, the most comprehensive published work about Dorland Robinson. Sue's interest in Dorland Robinson was piqued again when the Society mounted another exhibit of Dorland's artwork in 2003. Since then Sue has poured through old newspapers, searched census records, and written numerous letters to archives and individuals across the country seeking obscure facts about the people in Dorland's life, and locating artwork in private collections. Sue's contributions to this book are significant. The results of her fruitful efforts are greatly appreciated.

Public historian Richard Engeman; *Oregon Painters* co-author Ginny Allen; and Mark Humpal of Mark Humpal Fine Art each helped with Portland area research. In addition, Mark's familiarity with specific pieces of Dorland's artwork and his advice regarding art history and painting techniques was especially helpful. Others who assisted with the search for background information about Dorland include Betty Miller; Susan Davis; Julie Drengson of Jackson County Library Services, Medford Branch; Sister Sue Woodruff at Sisters of the Holy Names of Jesus & Mary Archives, Portland; Marian Yoshiki-Kovinick, formerly with Reference Services, Smithsonian Archives of American Art, West Coast Regional Center; Cheryl Leibold, Pennsylvania Academy of the Fine Arts Archivist; and of course Southern Oregon Historical Society library and collections staff: Curator of Collections Suzanne M.M. Warner, Carol Harbison-Samuelson, Kathy Enright, Tina Reuwsaat, and Jan Wright.

Several individuals played key roles in the visual and textual presentation of Dorland's life and artwork: SOHS Executive Director John Enders and *A Lasting Impression* project coordinator Harley Patrick for their direction and editing, SOHS photographer Anthony DiMaggio, and Chris Molé of Chris Molé Design.

The Southern Oregon Historical Society gratefully acknowledges the financial contributions of Sol and Virginia Blechman and the Finninsula Foundation, Mark Humpal of Mark Humpal Fine Art, the Oregon Heritage Commission, and several anonymous donors whose generosity made this publication possible. In addition, the Society is sincerely appreciative of the many private collectors who allowed images from their collections to be included in this book and of the following individuals and organizations who have graciously donated one or more Dorland Robinson paintings to the Southern Oregon Historical Society's permanent collection: Aderah Elmer Hudon, Alfred S.V. Carpenter, Alice Becroft Mitchell, Bess Kenney Ballard, Carroll L. Bacigalupi, E.B. Hanley Jr., Gladys Van Dyke, Jane Snedicor, Jean W. Jester, JoAnne Mitchell Elias, Julia Opp Johnson, Kathryn Heffernan, Marion Bowen, Maude A. Ackley, Oregon State Board of Education, Robert Heffernan, Robertson Collins, Tresa Matlack, University of Oregon, and Virginia Bandy Bernard.

CONTENTS

FOREWORD

As an outsider to the museum world but a long-time resident of Southern Oregon, I thought I had a pretty fair idea of the holdings of the Southern Oregon Historical Society when I assumed the position of Executive Director in October 2002. Then I began delving more deeply into the Society's permanent collection, and I was stunned. The breadth and size of the collection is amazing, from Native American baskets to pioneer tools, from diaries to artwork, from wooden shoes to a fire engine. Touring the Society's White City storage facility – where many of the collection's most important artifacts are kept – is an experience that fills one with humility and wonder. During my first tour, I was amazed by the sheer number of artifacts, as well as the work that had been done over the years to maintain, preserve and, in many cases, restore those artifacts so they would be available to future generations. What impressed me the most was when then-Curator Steve Wyatt rolled back a series of moveable wooden panels holding dozens and dozens of paintings and other pieces of artwork. Without a doubt, the most impressive work was that of Dorland Robinson, the Jacksonville, Oregon prodigy whose life and work are the subjects of this book. Her charcoals, oils, and watercolors simply jumped out at me. The quality of her work is undeniable, and the fact that the Society has so many of this artist's works in its collection makes it that much more impressive.

There is the bust portrait of the artist's father, who had arrived in Jacksonville in 1875 and who gave the portrait to a Medford woman. The painting was given to the Society in 1955. There is the watercolor of a masted sailing ship flying a French flag. It was given to the Society in 1957. There is a still life of a basket of fruit, given to SOHS in 1958. Or a portrait of a young girl seated at a table leafing through a book. That girl later donated the work to SOHS in 1960. There are so many. Over the years, many owners of Dorland Robinson paintings and sketches donated their precious belongings to the Society, trusting that SOHS would care for them, display them, preserve and, if needed, restore them.

In 1978, more than 30 of Dorland's works came to the Society from the University of Oregon, converting what had been a loan to a gift and approximately doubling the size of the Society's collection of Robinson works. Since then, other works have come to us from private donors. Art reviewers and experts have long commented on the astonishing ability of this young artist, and her ability to adapt different styles that she was studying. You don't really see that until you view many of her works side by side. When you do, her gift is inescapable. My reaction was to begin planning for a Dorland Robinson exhibit unlike any we'd had before.

Within days SOHS staffers were planning a major exhibit of Dorland's work. By the end of November we had decided to install that exhibit in the downstairs museum space of the Society's History Center building in downtown Medford, Oregon. The exhibit was a great success, and by April 2003 we were discussing the future publication of a book on the life and work of Dorland Robinson. What you see is the product of those talks, and many months of planning and work by the author, those who assisted her, and the professional, hard-working staff at SOHS.

This book is not only the product of those who worked on it, but also is the product of many years of preservation work by the Southern Oregon Historical Society. In addition, we at SOHS owe much to those over the years who have entrusted to us the works that you see in this book. We hope you enjoy this publication now and for many years to come.

John Enders
Executive Director
Southern Oregon Historical Society

Undated watercolor on paper. Private collection.

NEARLY A CENTURY HAS PASSED SINCE DORLAND'S DEATH, YET SOME-
THING OF HER ESSENCE LIVES ON THROUGH HER ART. REGINA DORLAND
ROBINSON HAS INDEED LEFT A LASTING IMPRESSION. HER SKETCHES AND
PAINTINGS CONTAIN AN IMMEDIACY THAT STIRS THE IMAGINATION
AND HER SOFT IMPRESSIONISTIC TOUCH INSPIRES AN ADMIRATION
THAT TRANSCENDS TIME.

Introduction

*Young Dorland, cherished by
her parents, was pampered and
indulged. SOHS Photo #487.*

FOR MOST OF HER BRIEF LIFE, Regina Dorland
Robinson worked steadily toward one goal: to
become an accomplished and successful artist.
She studied and practiced technique, experi-
menting with multiple mediums and styles. By
1916, at the age of twenty-four, she had gained a
confidence and competency that gave her work
its inspiring uniqueness. Dorland was receiving
recognition for her work, not only in her home
state of Oregon but also around the San Fran
cisco Bay Area—a major center of West Coast
art. The following year, in the spring of 1917, she
took her own life. How could she come so close
to achieving her life's dream only to end it so abruptly? And why?

Born in 1891 in the small Southern Oregon town of Jacksonville,
Dorland grew up in an impressive three-story home overlooking the
Rogue River Valley. Beautiful and talented, Dorland became a cherished but overly protected little girl. Her parents, Dr. James and Matilda
Robinson, were prominent citizens in the community. To keep their
daughter from harm, the Robinsons kept close rein on her activities,
sent her to a private school, and carefully chose her playmates.

Dorland's first exposure to art came in her own home where
ornately framed landscapes adorned the parlor walls. Her father was an
amateur painter, and a family friend, photographer Peter Britt, also was
an artist. Dorland no doubt learned something about painting early
on from both men and showed artistic potential at a young age. Her
eighth grade drawings, part of a class assignment, reveal an untrained
yet remarkable ability.

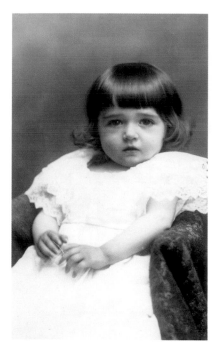

Earliest known photo of Dorland, ca. 1894. SOHS Photo #13201.

As an adolescent, Dorland spent countless hours drawing and painting. Recognizing her exceptional talent, Dorland's parents provided art lessons in Northern California, Portland, Oregon, and at the prestigious Pennsylvania Academy of the Fine Arts.

By the end of 1911, it was decided that, if Dorland's career were to flourish, she needed to relocate to a metropolitan area. The family chose Oakland, California. For the next several years, Dorland and her mother maintained a residence in California while her father traveled back and forth from Oregon. During this time, Dorland developed contacts within the San Francisco and East Bay art community and honed her impressionistic style. By 1915, the Robinsons were living once again in Jacksonville.

The year 1916 was undoubtedly the most eventful, and in some ways the most bizarre, year in Dorland's life. The artist's talent captured the attention of the ladies of the Greater Medford Club, a women's civic improvement group in Southern Oregon's largest community. In January, club members organized an elegant tea and exhibition of Dorland's paintings. The affair was so successful that a second show was planned for the following year.

Dorland traveled to San Francisco in April, probably for the first time without a parent by her side. Her traveling companion was Mrs. G.E. Johnson from Medford who seemed to be known in Portland art and social circles. The two women spent three weeks visiting the enormous art exhibit held over from the 1915 Panama-Pacific International Exposition.

August brought more recognition to Dorland when she received praise and attention for a life-sized portrait of Mrs. Johnson that was exhibited at the Hotel Portland. By then arrangements were being made for Dorland's work to be shown at the Portland Art Museum in the fall.

The emerging young artist's prospects were bright. She was beginning to reap long sought rewards for her years of focused dedication when she stumbled onto a ruinous distraction.

The timing and details are frustratingly vague, but at some point, Dorland met Charles Henry Pearson, a salesman who lived in San Francisco. Dorland and Charles married in October of 1916 in Portland. Following the wedding, the bride and groom went traveling. Before the end of November, the newlyweds stopped briefly in Jacksonville before heading to San Francisco to make their home.

Then, unknown trouble struck. Newspaper accounts indicate Dorland suffered a nervous breakdown and that the couple was divorcing less than three months after they wed. By early 1917, Dorland's health improved and she and her mother took rooms at a boarding house in San Mateo, California. Twenty-five-year-old Dorland turned back to her art.

That March, Dorland displayed several new paintings at a nearby gallery. On April 5, Mrs. Johnson received a letter from Dorland inviting her to visit. Dorland seemed to be doing well, when suddenly her life was over. Obituaries described how, on April 7, 1917, Mrs. Robinson found her daughter lifeless in the bedroom; a revolver lay nearby. Dorland was buried in Jacksonville a few days later.

Nearly a century has passed since Dorland's death, yet something of her essence lives on through her art. Regina Dorland Robinson has indeed left a lasting impression. Her sketches and paintings contain an immediacy that stirs the imagination and her soft impressionistic touch inspires an admiration that transcends time.

Dorland at age 15 or 16. Photographed at the Aune Studio in Portland, Oregon. Dorland studied art in Portland between 1907-08. It is likely that this portrait was taken during that time. SOHS Photo #488.

MUCH OF WHAT WE KNOW ABOUT REGINA DORLAND ROBINSON'S
LIFE IS SHROUDED IN MYSTERY AND FILLED WITH HALF-ANSWERED
QUESTIONS. MOST OF WHAT IS DOCUMENTED COMES FROM SCANT
NEWSPAPER ITEMS, A FEW PHOTOGRAPHS, AND TAPED INTERVIEWS OF
A HANDFUL OF PEOPLE RECALLING IMPRESSIONS OF DORLAND MORE
THAN SIXTY YEARS AFTER HER DEATH.

Part One:
A PRIVATE LIFE

LOCAL STORIES, PASSED THROUGH SEVERAL GENERATIONS, have
created a mystique about Dorland's secluded life and her tragic end. It
is a common assumption that she was a loner, overly sheltered by doting
parents. Decades-old rumors and town gossip regarding Dorland's
romance and death hint at a dark secret that may or may not have
existed. Some versions doubt that Dorland really married and claim
she took her life because she was unwed and pregnant. Others assert
the marriage failed because of her naivety and inexperience with men.
Highly speculative innuendos cast her husband as a caddish villain
accusing him of bigamy, or suggesting he infected her with venereal
disease before abandoning her.[1] None of these stories is substantiated
and Dorland, of course, took the truth to her grave.

A recent search of vital statistics, government records, and various history and art history archives have shed a pencil-thin ray of new
light on previously unanswered questions, but much is still unknown.
No diary or suicide note has been discovered giving clues to Dorland's
inner thoughts. Five letters, old school papers, and a newspaper quote
hold Dorland's only known words. Several pages of memoirs from her
father provide basic facts, but little more. In spite of missing details,
enough information exists to place the evolution of Dorland's artwork
within the context of this intriguing young woman's short life.

Adding to the romance of Dorland's compelling story is the
fact that she was raised by parents of pioneer stock in the historic
Gold Rush town of Jacksonville, Oregon. Once a thriving commer-
cial center, Dorland's hometown was by-passed by the railroad in the
1880s. Although it remained the county seat until 1927, Jacksonville

ABOVE: *Dorland Robinson,
ca.1903. SOHS Photo #15889.*

LEFT: *Portrait of Dorland's
cousin, Margaret Kubli (Robinson).
Watercolor and gouache on paper;
dated 1907; 12 x 9 inches. Private
collection (see page 35).*

Dr. James W. Robinson, Dorland's father. SOHS Photo #4531.

Mary Leah (l) and Willie Cecil (r) Robinson, Dorland's sister and brother. SOHS Photo #13009.

lost its economic base and stayed a quaint little village trapped in the past by its own history. Even today, the predominant architecture of Jacksonville is distinctively 19th century. Most of the community is designated a National Historic Landmark District.

Both sets of Dorland's grandparents journeyed by covered wagon over the Oregon Trail. Dorland's father, James William Robinson, was born on a donation land claim near Portland in 1850. After attending Oregon's first medical school at Willamette University in Salem, he came to Jacksonville to be a country doctor in 1878. Robinson married a classmate, who was also a doctor. She took ill and died within eight months of the wedding. Three years later, Dr. Robinson married Sarah Matilda (Tillie) Miller, Dorland's mother.

Tillie was a baby when her German immigrant parents, John and Mary Miller, crossed the plains and settled in Jacksonville in 1860. John acquired mining and orchard property and built a profitable gunsmith and hardware business in the bustling young community.

A number of German speaking families from Prussia, Switzerland, and Germany made Jacksonville their home. Although they integrated well with their non-German speaking neighbors and often took on civic leadership roles, they also formed fraternal groups and life-long friendships based on their common cultural heritage. Tillie's family had such a relationship with the family of Peter Britt. Britt had been an itinerant artist in Switzerland and became a renowned photographer in Oregon. The families seem to have been close. Long after Peter Britt's death in 1905, Tillie and her husband continued their association with Britt's son and daughter, Emil and Molly.[2]

The Millers stood well in the community. Tillie Miller and her six siblings mixed with the most refined and respectable young ladies and gentlemen in Jacksonville society. Although not Catholic, Tillie attended the local St. Mary's Academy. In her youth she sang or played guitar at community socials but after marrying, she appears to have withdrawn into her home, devoting herself to family, reading circle meetings, choir, and other Presbyterian Church activities.[3] Dorland's father was well situated with both a medical practice and a drugstore. He sat on the town council and served at least one term as mayor. Dorland was from a family with influence and reputation.

The Robinsons had two children before Dorland. Willie Cecil and Mary Leah were six and five years old, respectively, in 1890 when they died, less than one week apart, of diphtheria. Few facts are known about Dorland's older siblings. A statue of a kneeling child marks their graves. Little remains from their short existence—just a few charming photographs and birth and death announcements pasted in a family scrapbook.[4] It is often said this tragedy is why the Robinsons so indulged and guarded their third child who was born a year after the shocking loss.

Within weeks of Dorland's birth on November 5, 1891,[5] workers began building the spacious and well-furnished home where Dorland was raised.[6] As she grew older and began her art career, Dorland's parents provided an art studio at the house. While a grandson of the Robinson's next-door neighbor described the studio as a "flat-roofed square building" between the two houses.[7] Mabel Reeve (Vroman), who posed for Dorland in 1909, remembered the "arts room" as "a little room in her home … it was very neat." Mabel said the space opened into the back porch where the two girls played with kittens during a break.[8]

It appears that Dorland also had the use of Peter Britt's studio after he died. Albert Mitchell, another local resident that Dorland drew posed as a newspaper boy, stated that his portrait was done at the Britt house.[9]

A sketch of Britt's studio (see page 65) done on the same type of light blue paper used for Albert's portrait (see page 17) lends credence to this story.

Dorland's house faced the old stagecoach road that led north out of town and had a commanding view of scattered fields and farmsteads in the spreading valley below. The young artist frequently left her studio to paint or draw outdoor scenes including several that she did along this country lane. One life-long Jacksonville resident, about seven years younger than Dorland, remembered passing the Robinson's house on her way to school: "It was such a common occasion to have her sitting with her easel and little frame out along Old Stage Road there, painting … sometimes it was close in town, sometimes it was clear on out quite a ways down the road …." [10]

Sarah Matilda (Tillie) Miller Robinson, Dorland's mother. SOHS Photo #8981.

Although Dorland lived on the outskirts of town, it was a short walk to her father's drug store where she spent time. Dorland could have easily strolled to her Grandmother Miller's house or visited her Uncle John at the post office where he was postmaster.

Jacksonville residents remembered Dorland as a lonely girl without companions. During interviews, they made remarks such as "... she was an only child and pretty much of a recluse" and "… she seemed so alone all the time, as if she had no friends."[11] In contrast to these impressions, however, there is evidence that Dorland did have friends and even participated in community events.

When Dorland was about ten or eleven she played with Louise Williamson (Issacs), a neighbor girl who lived several blocks closer to town. Occasionally Dorland brought a basket of "tiny buttered biscuits" to Louise's house and the two girls played "old-fashioned, out-of-doors games such as 'run sheep run' and 'hide and go seek.'" Louise recalled

that Dorland "was friendly and happy as a playmate," and that "she wanted to have fun." Characterizing Dorland as "quiet if she did not know you," even Louise suggested that Dorland did not play with other children.[12]

Like her mother, Dorland attended classes at St. Mary's Academy. While children at the public school would not have had much opportunity to know Dorland, the young artist would have been well acquainted with the student body at her own small private school.

The Robinson's house was built in 1891 but burned down in the 1930s. Next door, the Nunan House, a well-known Jacksonville landmark, was untouched and still stands. Both houses were built from plans ordered through architect George F. Barber's catalog, "The Cottage Souvenir." SOHS Photo #829.

One schoolmate, Anna Kasshafer (Rumley), remembered visiting Dorland at her home to have a portrait done. "Dorland and I were great friends," Anna said, "… she was just a fine person."[13]

Dorland developed a deep friendship with three sisters from the Neil family. Nydah, who was the same age as Dorland, and Mildred, two years older, studied with Dorland at St. Mary's. The sister's grandparents lived across the street from the Robinsons. In 1900, when the girls were ten and eight years old, they lived there too, along with their mother and baby sister.[14]

Four letters written by Dorland to Mildred in 1912 and 1913, and one written to the youngest sister, Carol Frances, in 1916[15] (see Appendix Two),

indicate that the girls communicated regularly and that Dorland maintained a friendship with the family. Mildred visited Dorland and her mother at their temporary home in Oakland, California, and afterwards, sent photographs taken during their excursion to San Francisco's Knob Hill and Golden Gate Park. A discussion of a photography book Dorland had read in Philadelphia, written by a leading New York photographer, indicates a

Dorland on the staircase of her spacious home. SOHS Photo #828.

common interest between the two young women. In the letter written to Frances during the summer of 1916, Dorland recalled her recent visit to the Neil family ranch near Butte Falls, Oregon.

In spite of her retiring nature, Dorland is known to have participated in several public musical events. While a pupil at St. Mary's,

she performed in school presentations. In 1904, Dorland portrayed a lady in waiting in an operetta called *The Golden Slipper*. She also played instrumental duets for the 1904 and 1905 commencement ceremonies and in 1908, at seventeen, she played a piano solo at a library benefit.[16] How often Dorland stepped out in mixed company is not known, but in 1915, a local paper listed her among a dozen young men and women who attended a "500 Club" card party.[17]

This 1914 view shows Dr. Robinson's drugstore (second building from the right) in the center of Jacksonville's business district. SOHS Photo #20120.

It is often alleged that Dorland's absorption with her art left little time for socializing, but with Alice Becroft, another aspiring artist, Dorland found common ground. By 1915, Dorland was acquainted with Alice, who purchased art supplies at Dr. Robinson's drug store.[18] Alice had studied art in high school and showed potential. Dorland encouraged her and may have inspired her to seek formal training later at the Otis Art Institute in Southern California. In 1919, Alice married Albert Mitchell, one of Dorland's earlier models. In a 1980 interview, Albert recalled that during the time the two young women were friends, Alice painted portraits of Dorland and her father. Alice and Albert were given several of Dorland's paintings, which they displayed in their home.[19]

Dorland's uncle, Postmaster John Miller, tended the Jacksonville post office and family hardware store seen behind this 1907 Buick touring car. SOHS Photo #10368.

Of all Dorland's known acquaintances, most fascinating was her 1916 traveling companion. Acknowledged in contemporary news articles only as Mrs. G.E. Johnson, for decades her identity was unknown, and many wondered who she was and why Dorland's parents trusted her with their daughter. Only recently has part of this puzzle been pieced together.

City directories showed Mrs. G.E. Johnson was Stella, wife of George Johnson, chief clerk and general manager for the Spokane, Portland, and Seattle Railroad. The couple lived in Portland between 1909 and 1915. They then moved to Medford where George became

The Palace of Fine Arts where Dorland and Stella enjoyed the 1916 Post Panama-Pacific Art Exhibition in San Francisco. SOHS Collection #917.9461.

The most haunting questions in Dorland's story are those raised by her ill-fated marriage and premature death. When and where Dorland met Charles Henry Pearson is hinted at in one of several news items announcing their marriage: "The romance began in San Francisco during the World's Fair and culminated in Portland, where Miss Robinson was painting a portrait."[24] Most likely, this statement refers to Dorland's visit with Stella Johnson to the Post Panama-Pacific Art Exhibition in the spring of 1916 rather than the actual International Exposition that Dorland and her parents attended the previous summer.[25]

superintendent for the Pacific & Eastern Railroad.[20] A 1917 newspaper article mentioning Mrs. Johnson's ailing father provided her maiden name, which led to contact with a family member.

Stella Shaule Johnson was eleven years older than Dorland and a fellow artist. Although the mother of two young boys (ages seven and twelve in 1916), she was able to get away for extended trips. Shortly after arriving in Medford, Stella helped found the Medford Arts and Crafts League, a "department" of the Greater Medford Club.[21]

How Stella and Dorland met is still unknown. Stella undoubtedly attended Dorland's January 1916 art show in Medford. She may have been one of the organizers. It has been suggested that there was a connection between Stella and the Neil girls. Maybe they introduced the two women.[22] Whatever brought Stella and Dorland together, their relationship apparently was built upon a keen interest in art, and their trip together to San Francisco had a significant impact upon the course of Dorland's life. (Following Dorland's death, Stella continued to pursue her own art career as a painter and sculptor. Samples of her oil landscapes painted between 1903 and 1942 show a fondness for bright colors. Although good, they do not compare in quality to Dorland's work and Stella's style had a harder edge.)[23]

Upon returning from the California excursion, Stella told a reporter they "met many delightful people in the art circles of San Francisco which added much pleasure to our visit."[26] Unknown is whether Charles was part of this group. Aside from his career with the Yale Lock Company, little is known about his background or what drew him into this stratum of society. Was Dorland introduced to Charles through an acquaintance? Or was their meeting an unrelated, yet fateful, chance encounter?

Although residing in San Francisco in 1916, thirty-seven-year-old Charles Pearson was from New York City. His family seems to have been middle-class and respectable. The federal census shows that he received some schooling after high school and had already started a career in the hardware business by 1910. He was, at that time, living with his parents and siblings on Manhattan's West 95th Street. His father was a telegrapher, one brother was a salesman for an auto supply store, and the other was an office clerk. Both sisters had been teachers, but by 1910 one was married to a stockbroker and the other worked as a stenographer. Charles had also served as an officer during the Spanish-American War.

Dorland married Charles Pearson, twelve years her senior, on October 25, 1916 at the Congregational Church in Portland. The marriage, however, did not last.

The Superior Court of California in San Francisco County issued an interlocutory decree of divorce January 9, 1917. Charles actually started the process, filing for divorce December 13. The following day a news item in a Medford paper indicated Dorland was seriously ill in a Bay Area hospital.[27] By early January, Dorland was out of the hospital and recovering.[28] She filed for divorce on a cross-complaint January 6 and the provisional decree was granted three days later. The decree found Pearson guilty of "extreme cruelty" and the "wrongful infliction of grievous mental suffering." Both were standard complaints for the time. Unfortunately, civil records over thirty years old were destroyed as a matter of policy. Therefore, there is no testimony detailing the couple's troubles. The divorce was never finalized because Dorland died during the required waiting period, although she did resume using her maiden name and was listed as single instead of divorced on her death certificate.[29]

It is not known where Charles was when Dorland took her life, or how her death affected him. His military record shows that he was recalled to active duty in the Army in February 1918 and eventually shipped to Paris, France, for the duration of World War I.[30] After the War, he returned to the family home in Manhattan and resumed his work with the Yale Lock Co.

There is no evidence that Charles ever took another wife. He is listed as a "widower" in the 1930 census, which would be correct since the divorce was not final. By that time, he was fifty-one years old, his parents were dead, and he was boarding with one of his brothers and a sister across the East River in Jackson Heights. Information supplied on his death certificate by a nephew indicated Charles was single. Quite possibly the nephew never knew about Dorland.

Where Charles was in the 1940s and early 1950s is not known. In 1954, he moved into a modern urban redevelopment complex in Manhattan's lower east side. There he remained until his death in 1968 at the age of 89.[31]

Black and white studio photograph of Dorland's last self-portrait. The location of the original color pastel, signed "Dorland Robinson" and dated 1917, is unknown. SOHS Photo #489.

Details about Dorland's suicide are limited to contemporary newspaper accounts and her death certificate,[32] which attributed cause of death to a gunshot wound "committed by her own hand while temporarily deranged, suicidal." Explanations in the press center on Dorland's "unhappy domestic experience" and exhaustion from "overwork at her art" too soon after her attack of 'nervous prostration.'" Although the facts of one's life can be retrieved, their emotions cannot. Who can fully understand what carried Dorland to such a desperate place that she found the prospect of life unbearable? Those who look back and ask "why" will have to settle for an explanation given in a Medford paper: "Miss Robinson was but a child, of an unusually sensitive and intense disposition, and could not throw off disappointments as readily as a less temperamental person." [33]

DORLAND ROBINSON WAS A GIFTED AND PROLIFIC ARTIST. FOR JUST A DOZEN YEARS, BETWEEN HER EARLY TEENS AND THE TIME OF HER DEATH AT AGE TWENTY-FIVE, SHE PRODUCED A SURPRISING NUMBER OF PAINTINGS AND SKETCHES IN A VARIETY OF STYLES. IT IS ESPECIALLY FORTUNATE THAT ENOUGH PIECES SURVIVE FROM DIFFERENT PERIODS OF HER LIFE AND STAGES OF TRAINING, THAT HER MATURATION AND STYLISTIC DEVELOPMENT CAN BE CLEARLY OBSERVED.

Part Two:
AN ENDURING TREASURE

THE EARLIEST EXAMPLES OF DORLAND'S ART include several finely executed pen and ink drawings incorporated into handwritten eighth grade essays (see page 91).[34] The proficiency and detail of these illustrations show Dorland's potential. Recognizing her innate talent, Dorland's parents provided the art education and support she needed to become a professional artist.

Although Dorland may have experimented with oil paint while still in grade school, her first formal art training probably began in California when she was fifteen years old. According to a November, 1906 *Medford Mail* newspaper article, the Robinson family planned to spend the winter in Berkeley where Dorland would take painting instructions from "competent tutors." In March 1907, the same paper announced the family's return from Pacific Grove on the Monterey Peninsula. Because of the differing reports, it is unclear where Dorland took her lessons. Either town was a likely location for instruction because San Francisco artists displaced by the 1906 earthquake were relocating to both California coastal communities at the time.[35]

Through early lessons with gouache, or opaque watercolor, Dorland learned to draw her subjects in pencil and color them with the poster-paint-like pigment. The approach was more illustrative than interpretive. After returning to Jacksonville in the spring, Dorland painted a full-length self-portrait and copied from a black and white engraving, a clever genre scene of a horse pulling an automobile. At this time, Dorland began painting portraits of children from life. These pictures were charming and skillfully done, but were generally flat profiles and lacked the depth of form she would soon master.[36]

ABOVE: *Self-portrait. Oil on canvas, signed "R.D. Robinson"; no date; 23 1/2 x 15 3/4 inches. SOHS Collection #B412.*

LEFT: *This view of Jacksonville in the snow was painted after a January 1916 snowstorm. Oil on canvas. Private collection (see page 73).*

In 1907, Dorland began receiving public acknowledgement for her work. That August, her portrait of six-year-old Dorothy Metschan (see page 34) was published in a Portland paper, the *Oregon Journal.*[37] The accompanying article told of another portrait she had done of Oregon Governor George Chamberlain while he made a Fourth of July speech. "Miss Regina finished the sketch in colors, and forwarded it to Governor Chamberlain, who was so impressed with the little maiden's work he wrote her a personal letter complimenting her...." That fall, Dorland's nature sketches won first place at the Grants Pass Industrial Fair.[38]

Encouraged by the recognition, Dorland's parents took her to Portland where she studied oil painting and life drawing under the direction of Boston artist Florence Chase Currier, at the Oregon School of Art.[39] Here Dorland's true talent burst forth as she produced an astonishing series of dramatic charcoal drawings. The posed figures are engaging—a melancholy young woman sitting on a stool, a cowboy standing tall, a Turk dressed in native costume. These subjects appear to be professional models in a classroom or studio setting. Although the sketches are undated, others of equal caliber and style drawn after Dorland returned to Jacksonville are dated 1908 and 1909, giving a time context to the studies.

A Portland newspaper, the *Oregon Sunday Journal*, underscores Dorland's early painting

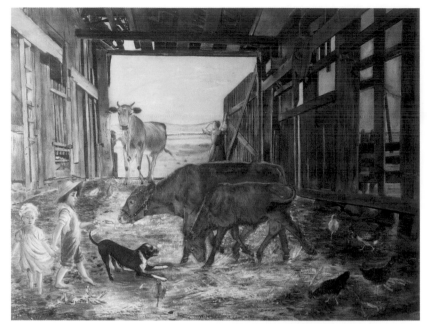

Three examples of Dorland's early work:

TOP: *"When the Cattle Come Home." Watercolor and gouache on paper; signed "Regina Dorland Robinson"; dated 1907; 19 1/2 x 25 1/2 inches. Perry Family Collection.*

ABOVE: *"Sure Thing." Gouache on paper; no date. SOHS Collection #1959.128.*

OPPOSITE PAGE: *Full-length self-portrait. Watercolor and gouache on paper; signed "Regina Dorland Robinson"; dated 1907; 28 x 11 1/2 inches. SOHS Collection #1978.20.32.*

ability. The paper reproduced a portrait Dorland painted of Judge George H. Williams, former Oregon Territory Chief Justice, U.S. Attorney General, and Portland Mayor. The accompanying article called Dorland a "prodigy" and stated that a pleased Williams "says it is the best that has ever been made of him." It took Dorland seven, one-hour sittings to complete the painting.[40]

Judge Williams was the law partner of C.E.S. Wood, another important Portland figure. Among other things, Wood was an enthusiastic arts patron and critic, and an amateur artist. Perhaps he met Dorland for the first time when she painted Williams. Wood acquired several of Dorland's paintings and thought highly of her work.[41] Looking at one of Dorland's pictures during a 1910 newspaper interview, he said, "For originality and breadth of treatment it is wonderful and unusual." A month before Dorland's death, a California paper quoted Wood as saying, "This young woman is undoubtedly a genius. Oregon should and doubtless will appreciate the fact." [42]

The Robinsons returned to Jacksonville sometime in 1908. During the rest of that year and throughout 1909, Dorland persuaded local residents to sit for portraits. It was during this time that she used Peter Britt's studio for some of her work.

Not all of Dorland's portraits were done indoors. Mabel Reeve (Vroman), who posed in Dorland's home studio, accompanied a friend, Ruthetta Ennis, when Dorland sketched the Presbyterian minister's daughter on the Britt grounds. Mabel recalled how "Ruthetta set out on a limb, the limb kind of went out from the little ditch, and she sat there and Dorland sketched her. I was just watching." [43] Another one of Dorland's models, Bernice Myer (Hicks), recalled going with Dorland on sketching excursions along Ashland Creek.

Dorland and her parents stayed with Bernice's family when they attended the summer Chautauqua in Ashland, Oregon. Chautauqua was a national movement that brought cultural and educational programs to small towns and rural areas across America. For two weeks in July, thousands of people from nearby communities camped or

filled hotels and boarding houses while they enjoyed lectures, music, dancing, and other entertainment in Ashland's Chautauqua Tabernacle.[44]

While the audience watched the program, Dorland sketched the audience. Bernice described Dorland and her actions: "Dorland was always a girl unto herself…her whole life and thought was paint, paint, paint. She would take her sketchbook with her at the Chautauqua and on one of these little

As this melancholy charcoal demonstrates, by age sixteen Dorland already had a remarkable ability to convey strong emotion through her drawings. Charcoal on paper; signed "Dorland Robinson"; no date; 24 3/4 x 18 3/4 inches. SOHS Collection #1979.26.5.

This drawing of a model dressed as a cowboy and the sketch of the woman on the left are both presumed to be class studies done at the Oregon School of Art in Portland. Charcoal on paper; signed "Dorland Robinson"; no date; 23 1/2 x 17 1/2 inches. SOHS Collection #1978.20.28.

penny tablets…she'd sit there and sketch everybody. And then she'd bring it home and Mother would look through it and tell her who everyone was." [45] In July 1908, Dorland drew John Sharp Williams, then-Democratic minority leader of the U.S. House of Representatives, while he gave an hour-and-a-half Chautauqua presentation.[46]

Placing Dorland's paintings in context is more challenging than sequencing her drawings. Many paintings are undated. Her early works show variety and experimentation. A series of oil landscapes and interiors, probably painted in Southern Oregon before Dorland studied in Pennsylvania, feature soft edges and a palette of bright pastels. Several of these, muted with a wash or glaze, incorporate more somber tones in the background. Two others, done pre-1910, are strikingly different. An interior of the

Atiyeh Brothers Oriental rug shop in Portland (see page 20) and a portrait titled "The Turk" (see page 21) are powerfully crafted with richly saturated reds and yellows. The revealing 1908 date on this signed portrait indicates it was done while Dorland was taking her Portland lessons. The man in Turkish dress appears to be the same model that posed in Dorland's sketch class. Both painting and sketch are exceptional for a sixteen-year-old.

Many of Dorland's still life oils are dark and heavy, reminiscent of the Munich style of painting. A number of these ceramic and metal groupings may have been student work done at the Pennsylvania Academy of the Fine Arts (PAFA). In sharp contrast, it appears Dorland developed a light and fluid approach for floral still life watercolors at the Academy.

Around 1908 or 1909, Dorland sketched young Albert Mitchell posed as a paperboy in Peter Britt's studio. Charcoal on light blue paper; signed "Albert Mitchell by Dorland Robinson"; no date; 23 3/4 x 17 1/4 inches; SOHS Collection #1957.114.4.

Mabel Reeve (Vroman) posed in Dorland's home studio. She recalled Dorland adjusting her dress, telling her where to put her feet, and to look toward her. The sitting took three days, about two hours each day. Charcoal on light blue paper; signed "Dorland Robinson"; dated 1909; 23 3/4 x 17 3/4 inches. SOHS Collection #1978.20.21.

Newspaper accounts show the Robinsons leaving for the East in late September 1910 and returning to Jacksonville in May 1911.[47] A registration card proves Dorland attended PAFA during that time, but does not specify her coursework. Theoretically, as a first year student, she would have taken cast drawing taught by Thomas Anshutz and still life painting taught by either Joseph T. Pearson or Hugh Breckenridge. Dorland could have also attended weekly lecture classes on anatomy with Dr. George McClellan, and one on perspective taught by architect Frank Miles Day.[48]

Dorland's training at PAFA was pivotal. From nine to five o'clock, she was immersed in instruction and studio work. Her tutors were highly experienced artists who had trained in both the United States and Europe. Dorland spent time viewing the master-

pieces of leading American painters displayed in the museum gallery above her classrooms. The experience gave Dorland broad exposure to diverse artistic influences, which she would adapt and meld into her own personal style.

After returning to Jacksonville, Dorland created some of her most fascinating work. Mixing watercolor and pastel, she painted ethereal arrangements of fresh spring and summer flowers. With oils, she captured Rogue Valley farm scenes in soft shades of rosy-beige and blues. From this time on, Dorland's artwork had a freer, more spontaneous, and relaxed sense to it. Her pieces are more suggestive with less attention to detail.

Dorland did not stay long in Jacksonville. In December, the Robinsons left for Oakland, Califor-

Landscape, presumed to have been done before Dorland trained at the Pennsylvania Academy of the Fine Arts. Oil on canvas; no date; 10 1/4 x 15 3/4 inches. SOHS Collection #1987.7.1.

Yams and turnips, still life. May have been done as a student work at the Pennsylvania Academy of the Fine Arts. It is representative of a number of Dorland's darker compositions. The brass pitcher to the right appears in several of her other paintings. Oil on canvas; signed "R.D. Robinson"; no date; 23 3/4 x 30 inches. SOHS Collection #1978.20.33.

nia, to launch Dorland's professional career. The family stayed in a large craftsman-style bungalow and quickly made connections in the art community. Twenty-year-old Dorland joined the Sketch Club, a long established art organization whose members included some of the most influential avant-garde artists in the Bay Area such as Anne Bremer, Arthur and Lucia Mathews, Geneve Rixford Sargeant, and Xavier Martinez.[49] By April 1912, Dorland had five pictures on exhibit at the San Francisco Art Association's spring exhibition.[50] A long article about Dorland in the *Oakland Tribune* reported that her paintings were "attracting the greatest attention from well-known critics across the bay." The paper called one landscape oil "charming, full of spirit, of soul...bearing the impress of the true artist...." A wealthy Oakland businessman purchased another painting titled, "Morning Through a Window." *The Tribune* described this work in detail: "One sees the sunlight streaming through a window and in it there is such feeling, such warmth, such color, that the spirit of sunlight dances in the sunbeams, and the picture stirs something unusual in the depths of one's heart and illumines life as well as the room into which it shines." [51]

In 1913, Dorland displayed two more paintings in the Art Association's annual show, and probably exhibited elsewhere in the Bay Area over the next few years.

Icons of the Northern California countryside—golden grassy

"Nasturtiums." Less than a year after it was painted, Dorland exhibited this still life at the Annual Spring exhibition of the San Francisco Art Association in April 1912. Later, in 1916, she displayed the painting at the Holland Hotel in Medford. Mixed media of watercolor over pastel on paper; signed "Regina Dorland Robinson"; dated 1911; 11 3/4 x 19 inches; SOHS Collection #1978.20.10.

hills and churning ocean surf—appear in Dorland's repertoire of paintings. Depictions of windswept Monterey Cypress suggest that Dorland and her family ventured to the Monterey Peninsula where an artists' colony had recently emerged. Dorland wrote in a 1912 letter to Mildred Neil that she and her mother did not travel much when her father was in Oregon. Presumably, excursions to paint surrounding landscapes were done only when Dr. Robinson was present.

Details about Dorland's formative time in Oakland are few. She undoubtedly had opportunities to meet and study with foremost painters who were defining the contemporary art scene. Dorland's later works show their influence in subject matter and style. Other than Alice Chittenden,[52] from whom Dorland took lessons in 1916, her mentors are unknown.

While Dorland lived in the Bay Area, promoters began planning the Panama-Pacific International Exposition. The World's Fair, designed to celebrate the completion of the Panama Canal and San Francisco's comeback from the 1906 earthquake and fire, would include an ambitious art exhibit by modern European and American masters. Many leading California artists would also show their work.[53] By the time the exposition opened in 1915, Dorland was back in Oregon, but returned with her parents to see the fair that summer. When Dorland and Stella Johnson visited San Francisco together the following spring, they spent three weeks studying the art exhibition held over after the International Exposition closed.

After viewing the exhibition, Dorland told a newspaper journalist:

"I would scarcely know where to begin to describe the thousands and thousands of masterpieces by the greatest artists of the world … To study those indescribable pictures, for hours at a time, is not a task that fatigues; it is an intellectual feast. There were the products of the genius of the great masters of the world in every conceivable form of beauty and grandeur. We visited the galleries every day and remained for hours at a time. I will be forever grateful for the opportunity of studying that great variety of artwork.

"I was fascinated with the outdoor work of Spencer and Metcalf and with the still life of William M. Chase. These are our greatest artists in those lines, I believe, in America. I filled three or four notebooks with observations noted while studying their work. I never crowded so much real pleasure into three weeks of time before in my life."[54]

The newspaper also explained that the two women attended several art lectures during their stay, and made a large number of sketches of the people and sights they saw on their trip. Today, the location of these sketches and Dorland's notes is unknown.

While establishing herself in California art circles, Dorland maintained ties to Oregon. She and her mother made sporadic trips north, and during the times she was in Jacksonville, she painted more local scenes and portraits. By 1916, Dorland was receiving significant exposure in Medford and Portland.

Regina Dorland Robinson

ABOVE: *"The Turk." Judging from the 1908 date on this portrait, and the location of the Atiyeh Brothers rug shop, it is presumed that Dorland created both pictures while studying art in Portland at the Oregon School of Art. Oil on canvas; signed "Regina Dorland Robinson"; dated 1908; 25 x 16 inches. Private collection.*

LEFT: *A corner of the Atiyeh Brothers rug shop in Portland, Oregon. This painting received some water damage in the left bottom corner during a fire in the late 1980s or early 1990s. Oil on canvas; signed "Regina Dorland Robinson"; no date; 25 x 18 inches. Private collection.*

The one-woman show presented by the Greater Medford Club in January featured thirty-five of Dorland's paintings. An appreciative audience viewed the artwork at the stylish Holland Hotel. Two paintings sold that day and Dorland lined up several portrait commissions. A number of Dorland's ethereal still life watercolors done in 1911 were shown along with newer portraits, and several local scenes, including two painted after a snowstorm that month (see pages 72-73). In reporting the posh affair, a local newspaper called Dorland "an artist of unusual ability and promise," while another dubbed her a "genius." [55]

More attention was lavished on Dorland that August when she showed a portrait of Stella Johnson in Portland. The life-size pastel hung in the parlor of the Hotel Portland for a week while articles in major Portland papers raved about Dorland's talent. Elements in the picture reflected oriental influences popular at the time. Mrs. Johnson, dressed in a blue mandarin robe, relaxed in a wicker chair with a huge red lantern behind her head. *The Oregonian* described this image: "A happy combination of coloring and some fine light effects and good composition are added to the lifelike expression." A reporter for the *Portland Evening Telegram* was reminded of premier American artist John LaFarge "in the handling of the picture," although he thought Dorland was more daring with her use of

"Peach Blossoms." This undated painting, one of Dorland's later works, was probably created in the spring of 1915. It was displayed in January 1916 at the Holland Hotel in Medford. Oil on canvas; signed "R.D. Robinson"; no date; 11 x 14 inches. SOHS Collection #1978.20.4.

color.[56] One of the continuing mysteries of Dorland's story is the location of this "lost" portrait.

Portlanders saw more of Dorland's work in November at the Fifth Annual Exhibition of the Works of Artists of the Pacific Northwest. The show, sponsored by the Portland Art Association, was held at the Portland Art Museum. The four-week exhibition presented eighty-five pieces of artwork by thirty-five artists. Dorland's five oil paintings and one pastel were displayed in good company. Included in the exhibit were works by high profile artists such as C.E.S. Wood, Museum Curator Anna B. Crocker, and Museum Art School instructors Clara Jane Stephens, Helen Putnam, and Henry Wentz. Also among the exhibitors was impressionist painter Clyde Leon Keller who, like Dorland, was a native Oregonian who spent time with the Northern California artists.[57]

Dorland's final exhibit of artwork, just before her death in 1917, was at Crawford's Art Shop in Burlingame, California. The private gallery belonged to Dorothy Crawford, a prize-winning professional photographer, who frequently photographed San Francisco's society crowd. Here Dorland again displayed the large pastel of Stella Johnson along with a new self-portrait (see page 11). In an article publicizing this display, the *San Mateo County Times* described Dorland as "one of the most promising of the younger group of American artists…" and explained how her work showed "a rare feeling for form and color." The paper also told of two portraits recently completed. One, a life-size pastel of young singer Genevieve Holmberg Lyon, would be displayed at the local high school when Mrs. Lyon performed in concert. The other was of Dr. Archie L. Offield (see page 26) who attended Dorland in the hospital. Dr. Offield may have been given his portrait as payment for his service.[58]

Members of the Greater Medford Club were so thrilled by the success of their first showing of Dorland's artwork that they scheduled a second exhibit for April 1917. Ironically, a society column announcing the upcoming event ran in the same Medford newspaper that carried news of Dorland's suicide.[59]

In the years following Dorland's death, Dr. and Mrs. Robinson gave some of her paintings to family and close friends. Many were sold and others, like the Offield portrait, were possibly traded for services. After Mrs. Robinson died in 1931, Dr. Robinson moved to a hotel in Medford and then to a nursing home. He died in 1938. The Robinson's Jacksonville home burned sometime in the 1930s after Dr. Robinson moved out. By then most or all of Dorland's paintings had been removed.[60]

As a memorial to their daughter, Dr. and Mrs. Robinson donated a large collection of Dorland's paintings and drawings to the University of Oregon in 1922. The "Dorland Robinson Art Collection" was dedicated the next year at the opening of the University's new building for the School of Architecture and Allied Arts. For many years, Dorland's paintings were cared for and displayed by the university in Eugene.

In 1957, the University of Oregon loaned and later deeded the Dorland Robinson Collection to the Southern Oregon Historical Society because of the artist's historical ties to the region. This collection included early and later oils, pastels, and watercolors as well as a large portfolio of the 1908 and 1909 sketches. Other works donated by individuals added to the Southern Oregon Historical Society's collection, making it the largest compilation of Dorland Robinson artwork in existence.

Much of Dorland's artwork remains in private hands. Nearly fifty pieces have been located. A number of others are "lost" works, like Stella Johnson's portrait. Known only through an exhibition list or an old newspaper description, they may or may not have survived.

Surveying the exceptional body of work Dorland produced in just over a decade, it is easy to see her potential, and wonder what she might have done had she not died so young. Could she have been a major artist? Would she have found her way to the art conclaves in New York or Paris? How would she have adapted her styles as contemporary art trends changed?

Regardless of what might have been, Dorland Robinson left a unique and meaningful legacy. Her evocative still life watercolors, misty landscapes, and sensi-

This delightful watercolor was discovered by its current owner at a garage sale. She knew nothing about the artist at the time, but liked the painting. It may be one of five rose paintings exhibited at the Holland Hotel, Medford, Oregon, January 21, 1916. Watercolor on paper; signed "Regina Dorland Robinson"; date is unclear; 21 1/4 x 15 1/4 inches. Private collection.

tive portraits have an enduring poignancy as relevant today as when they were created nearly a century ago.

Part Three:
THE COLLECTION

A NOTE ABOUT THE ARTWORK:

The collection of images in this book is merely a sampling of Regina Dorland Robinson's total body of work. Selections range from her earliest paintings to her latest pastels in an attempt to show Dorland's professional growth and versatility. Measurements provide an appreciation for picture size but might not be exact. This information was collected from a variety of sources and measuring techniques may have varied slightly. Some measurements indicate the actual size of the artwork while most designate inside frame measurements. A few plates show less than the complete drawing or painting. Available photographs of some of the art pieces were cropped and in several instances, the mats of framed works obscured dates and signatures. In such cases, text about a painting or drawing may note information that does not appear on the published image.

Left:
Still life watercolor on paper. Private collection (see PLATE #28).

Portraits and Figures

Above: PLATE #1
Curiously, the only known portrait of Dr. Robinson, Dorland's father, appears to be unfinished.
Oil on canvas; no date; 15 3/4 x 10 3/4 inches. SOHS Collection #1955.76.

Left: PLATE #2
Dr. Archie Leonard Offield, the doctor who treated Dorland during her 1916 illness. The painting,
one of Dorland's last portraits, may have been given to Dr. Offield as payment for his medical services.
Pastel or chalk on canvas; signed "Regina Dorland Robinson"; dated 1917; 35 x 24 1/2 inches.
Archie L. Offield Family Collection.

PLATE #3
Katherine Kubli (Gordon). Katherine was Dorland's cousin, younger daughter of Kaspar and
Mollie Miller Kubli. Charcoal on paper; signed "Regina Dorland Robinson";
dated 1909; 15 x 11 inches. Private collection.

PLATE #4
Virginia Bandy. Pastel on paper; signed "R.D. Robinson"; dated 1916;
22 1/4 x 15 inches. SOHS Collection #1961.139.

PLATE #5
Ora Marie Stout (Niedermeyer), a Rogue Valley resident. Gouache on paper; signed "Dorland Robinson";
no date; 18 1/4 x 10 1/2 inches. SOHS Collection #1978. 20.30.

PLATE #6

This garden portrait of an unidentified woman holding a parasol is reminiscent of a theme commonly painted by West Coast artists of the time. Oil on canvas; no date; 15 3/4 x 13 3/4 inches. SOHS Collection #B301.

PLATE #7
Unidentified young woman. Oil on canvas; no date; 16 x 13 3/4 inches. SOHS Collection #B274.

PLATE #8
Mildred Neil, Dorland's close friend. Dorland wrote letters to Mildred and in 1912 Mildred visited Dorland in
Oakland, California. Dorland displayed this portrait at the Portland Art Museum during the Fifth Annual
Exhibition of the Works of Artists of the Pacific Northwest, November 14–December 10, 1916. Pastel on paper;
signed "Regina Dorland Robinson"; dated 1916; 29 3/4 x 21 3/4 inches.
SOHS Collection #1977.35.1.

PLATE #9

Dorothy Metschan (Hawley). Dorothy was the daughter of Phil and Velene Kubli Metschan, inlaws of Dorland's aunt, Mollie Kubli. Phil Metschan owned the Imperial Hotel in Portland, which is where the Robinson's stayed while Dorland studied art in 1907 and 1908. Dorland received recognition for her talent when a likeness of this image was published in a Portland newspaper, the *Oregon Sunday Journal,* August 25, 1907. Watercolor and gouache on paper; signed "Regina Dorland Robinson"; dated 1907; 14 x 11 inches.
Dorothy "Dinda" Hawley Mills Collection.

PLATE #10

Margaret Kubli (Robinson). Margaret was Dorland's cousin and the older daughter of Kaspar and Mollie Miller Kubli. When Margaret grew up, she married a Robinson who was no relation to Dorland. Watercolor and gouache on paper; signed "Regina Dorland Robinson"; dated 1907; 12 x 9 inches. Private collection.

Above: PLATE #11
Tillie Miller, Dorland's mother, in profile. This little portrait was found tucked into a diary that belonged to
Molly Britt. Pastel on paper; signed "Dorland Robinson"; no date; 5 1/4 x 3 1/2 inches.
SOHS Collection #1994.78.1.2.

Left: PLATE #12
"Grandma Miller." Mary Miller, Dorland's maternal grandmother.
Mixed media of pastel and watercolor on paper; no date; 15 x 12 inches. Private collection.

Dorland completed these portraits of Elizabeth Hanley and her two children, Edward Hanley Jr. and Katheryn Hanley (Heffernan), in 1916. The exceptionally large portrait of Mrs. Hanley is probably similar in size to the one of Stella Johnson. An August 16, 1916 *Medford Mail Tribune* article tells how Mrs. Hanley displayed her portrait for the first time during a reception she held in her Rogue Valley home. The reception was for Mrs. Chas. P. Chamberlain, daughter-in-law of former Oregon Governor and then-U.S. Senator George E. Chamberlain. The current owner of the portrait also has the dress and shoes that Mrs. Hanley wore when the portrait was painted.

Above: PLATE #13
Edward B. Hanley, Jr. and Katheryn E. Hanley (Heffernan), Rogue Valley residents.
Pastel on paper; signed "R.D. Robinson"; dated 1916; 33 x 26 inches. Private collection.

Left: PLATE #14
Elizabeth Reese Hanley. Pastel on paper; signed "Regina Dorland Robinson";
dated 1916; 60 x 36 inches. Private collection.

PLATE #15

"The Turk." The model appears to be the same man who posed for the charcoal portrait of the same name on the opposite page. It is presumed that Dorland created both pieces while studying at the Oregon School of Art in Portland. Oil on canvas; signed "Regina Dorland Robinson"; dated 1908; 25 x 16 inches. Private collection.

PLATE #16
"The Turk." Charcoal on paper; signed "R.D. Robinson"; no date; 23 1/2 x 17 1/2inches.
SOHS Collection #1978.20.27.

Above: PLATE #17
A lily pond at the Peter Britt estate was the setting for the plein air portrait on the opposite page. Peter's son Emil photographed Dorland at her easel along with three young girls who were present the day the portrait was painted. The girl standing at the corner of the pond is the one who posed for the portrait.
Emil Britt photograph, "Pond Lilies." SOHS Photo #6704.

Left: PLATE# 18
Girl sitting at a lily pond. Oil on canvas; signed "Regina Dorland Robinson"; no date; 18 x 14 inches.
Lloyd and Annette Shreeve Collection. Photograph of painting by FROZENIMAGEPHOTO.COM.

Still Lifes

Above: PLATE #19
Dorland underpainted the entire surface of this painting with gold. It is the only known
example of her work where she used this technique. Oil with gold under painting on canvas; signed
"Regina Dorland Robinson"; no date; 20 x 28 inches. Perry Family Collection.

Left: PLATE #20
Still life of irises. Oil on canvas; signed "Regina Dorland Robinson"; no date; 15 1/2 x 13 3/4 inches.
SOHS Collection #1962.246.

PLATE #21

The large brass pot featured in this still life is from the Britt estate and is currently part of the
SOHS Collection. Oil on canvas; signed "Regina Dorland Robinson"; no date; 16 x 24 inches.
SOHS Collection #1964.55.

PLATE #22

Dorland's parents gave this painting to Katheryn Hanley Heffernan as a wedding present. Dorland had done a pastel portrait of Katheryn and her brother when they were children in 1916 (see Plate #14). Oil on canvas; signed "Dorland Robinson"; no date; 13 3/4 x 19 3/4 inches. SOHS Collection 1958.112.2.

PLATE #23
"Nasturtiums." Exhibited at both the San Francisco Art Association in 1912 and the Holland Hotel in 1916.
Mixed media of watercolor over pastel on paper; signed "Regina Dorland Robinson";
dated 1911; 11 3/4 x 19 inches; SOHS Collection #1978.20.10.

PLATE #24
"A Salad." Exhibited at the Holland Hotel, Medford, Oregon, January 21, 1916. Watercolor on paper;
no date; 11 x 19 3/4 inches. SOHS Collection #1978.20.12.

PLATE #25

"Peaches." This picture was exhibited at the Holland Hotel, Medford, Oregon, January 21, 1916.
Mixed media of gouache and pastel on paper; no date; 9 x 11 1/4 inches. SOHS Collection #1978.20.25.

PLATE #26
Still life of daffodils. Watercolor on paper; no date; dimensions unavailable. Private collection.

Above: PLATE #27
"Dahlias" or "Cactus Dahlias." This may be one of two dahlia paintings
exhibited at the Holland Hotel, Medford, Oregon, January 21, 1916, and/or
displayed at the Portland Art Museum during the Fifth Annual Exhibition of the
Works of Artists of the Pacific Northwest, November 14–December 10, 1916. Watercolor on paper;
signed "Regina Dorland Robinson"; dated 1915; 9 1/2 x 20 inches. Sue Waldron Collection.

Right: PLATE #28
Still life of white gladiolas in a terra cotta pot. Watercolor on paper; signed "Dorland Robinson";
no date; 19 1/2 x 13 inches. Private collection.

Similar in subject matter and composition, these two still life paintings of apples show
Dorland's versatility with different mediums.

Above: PLATE #29
Stoneware jug with apples in the foreground. Oil on canvas; signed "Regina Dorland
Robinson"; no date; 12 x 14 inches. Lloyd and Annette Shreeve Collection.
Photo by FROZENIMAGEPHOTO.COM.

Left: PLATE #30
Two apples with a Chianti wine bottle. Watercolor on paper; signed "Regina Dorland
Robinson"; dated 1912; 17 1/2 x 11 inches. Flinn Family Collection.

PLATE #31

This depiction of a red rose or poppy is unlike most of Dorland's other work. Although it is unsigned, its provenance is strongly linked to Dorland. The painting is one of several given to Alice Becroft Mitchell by Dorland or her parents. Many years later, Alice Mitchell gave the painting to Dorland Offenbacher, a Jacksonville resident who had the same first name as the artist. Watercolor on paper; no date; 7 1/2 x 5 1/2 inches.
Dorland (Godward) Offenbacher Collection.

PLATE #32

"Yellow Roses." Exhibited at the Annual Spring Exhibition of the San Francisco Art Association, 1912, and the Holland Hotel, Medford, Oregon, January 21, 1916. Watercolor on paper; signed "Regina Dorland Robinson"; dated 1911; 20 x 13 1/4 inches. SOHS Collection #1978.20.34.

PLATE #33
Still life with onions. Oil on wood; signed "Dorland Robinson"; no date; 19 3/4 x 14 3/4 inches.
SOHS Collection #B228.

PLATE #34
Still life oil with yams and turnips. Oil on canvas; signed "R.D. Robinson";
no date; 23 3/4 x 30 inches. SOHS Collection #78.20.33.

Interiors

Above: PLATE #35
One of three paintings Dr. Robinson gave to his friend and physician, Dr. James C. Hayes, in the 1930s.
Oil on canvas; no date; 15 1/2 x 12 1/2 inches. Private collection.

Left: PLATE #36
The impressionist-expressionist style of this painting highlights Dorland's skilled use of color.
Oil on canvas; signed "Regina Dorland Robinson"; dated 1910-1914 (unreadable final digit);
20 3/4 x 13 1/2 inches. SOHS Collection #1978.20.3.

PLATE #37

An open door provides a unique perspective of this subject. Oil on canvas; signed "Regina Dorland Robinson";
no date; 23 3/4 x 15 1/2 inches. SOHS Collection #1979.26.9.

PLATE #38
Another of the three paintings Dr. Robinson gave to his friend and physician, Dr. James C. Hayes,
in the 1930s. Oil on canvas; no date; 23 1/2 x 19 1/2 inches. Private collection.

Above: PLATE #39
Peter Britt studio. Charcoal and pressed pigment crayon on light blue paper; signed
"Regina Dorland Robinson"; no date; 12 1/2 x 23 3/4 inches.
SOHS Collection #1979.26.3.

Left: PLATE #40
Table and chair in corner of a room. Oil on canvas; signed "Dorland Robinson";
no date; 15 1/2 x 11 1/4 inches. SOHS Collection #1978.20.9.

Landscapes and Animals

Above: PLATE #41
The old City Brewery was among the aging buildings that Dorland painted in her hometown of Jacksonville.
Veit Shutz made beer in the looming three-story structure from at least 1869 through the early 1890s.
Pastel on paper; signed "Regina Dorland Robinson"; no date; 11 1/4 x 15 3/4 inches. SOHS Collection #1983.5.3.

Left: PLATE #42
"Veit Shutz Brewery." By the time Dorland created this view of the brewery around 1916, it was abandoned
and falling into disrepair. Oil on canvas; no date; 18 x 24 inches. Flinn Family Collection.

PLATE #43
"The Farm." Watercolor on paper; signed "R. Dorland Robinson"; dated 1907;
9 x 11 1/2 inches. Private collection.

PLATE #44

"Table Rock." Dorland choose a well-known Rogue Valley landmark for this nature study.
Watercolor on paper; signed "Regina Dorland Robinson"; no date;
11 1/2 x 15 inches. Private collection.

PLATE #45
Saddle horse in a stable. Watercolor on paper; signed "Regina Dorland Robinson";
no date; 21 x 16 inches. Private collection.

PLATE #46
Girl with a colt. Oil on canvas; no date; measurements unknown. Private collection.

PLATE #47

"A Wintry Day, 1916" or "First Snow, 1916." This rural scene and the painting on the opposite page were painted after a January 1916 snowstorm. They were probably both exhibited at the Holland Hotel in Medford on January 21, 1916 and at the Portland Art Museum during the Fifth Annual Exhibition of the Works of Artists of the Pacific Northwest, November 14–December 10, 1916. Oil on canvas; signed "R.D. Robinson"; dated 1916; 15 x 16 inches. Private collection.

PLATE #48

"A Wintry Day, 1916" or "First Snow, 1916." Also known as "Jacksonville." The Orth and Brunner Buildings appear in the foreground and the Jackson County Courthouse can be seen in the upper right background. Oil on canvas; signed "…Robinson"; no date; 16 x 18 inches. Private collection.

PLATE #49

"Peach Blossoms." One of Dorland's later works, this landscape was probably painted in the spring of 1915.
It was displayed the following January at the Holland Hotel in Medford. The back of this canvas is lined with
a piece of older canvas bearing a partial painting of a watering can and terra cotta flowerpot. Oil on canvas;
signed "R.D. Robinson"; no date; 11 x 14 inches.
SOHS Collection #1978.20.4.

PLATE #50

"Almond Blossoms." Included in the Dorland Robinson Collection that Mr. and Mrs. Robinson donated to the University of Oregon in 1922, this post-Impressionist, tonalist painting is quite different from Dorland's other works. The trees in the foreground were created with slabs of paint and lack detail. The painting's style may suggest influences from some of the San Francisco Bay Area avant-garde artists. Oil on canvas; no date; 10 1/4 x 12 3/4 inches. SOHS Collection #1978.20.26.

PLATE #51

"Sunlight, Rogue River Valley." When this landscape was exhibited at the San Francisco Art Association's Spring Exhibition in 1912, the *Oakland Tribune* described it as "full of soul." The painting was also displayed during the January 1916 show at the Holland Hotel in Medford. It was probably the first of a series of moody tonalist paintings Dorland did in soft shades of rosy-beige and blues. Oil on canvas; signed "Regina Dorland Robinson"; no date; 10 x 9 3/4 inches. SOHS Collection #1978.20.1.

PLATE #52
Winter scene. Oil on canvas; signed "R.D. Robinson"; dated 1914;
13 3/4 x 10 3/4 inches. SOHS Collection #1978.20.6.

PLATE #53

"Aspen Trees." This scene has been identified as the Pelton Ranch at Fort Klamath, Oregon. Mrs. Josephine Orth Pelton, a Jacksonville native, was a long-time friend of the Robinson family. One month before Dorland's marriage, on September, 25, 1916, the *Medford Mail Tribune* reported that "Miss Regina Dorland Robinson accompanied Mr. and Mrs. Pelton to their home at Fort Klamath going via Crater Lake." It is plausible that Dorland created this drawing at that time. Pastel on paper; signed "Regina Dorland Robinson"; no date; 14 x 20 1/4 inches. SOHS Collection #1978.20.13.

PLATE #54
Oil on canvas; signed "R.D. Robinson"; dated 1915;
13 x 18 inches. Mark Humpal and Diane Zuhl Collection.

Above: PLATE #55
"Sand Dunes and Cypress, Monterey, California." Depicts a typical Monterey Peninsula
scene. Watercolor on paper; signed "Regina Dorland Robinson"; no date; 6 1/2 x 14 inches.
SOHS Collection #78.20.15.

Left top: PLATE #56
"Oh Why Don't Father Come?" This 1907 watercolor is typical of Dorland's early illustrative style. Watercolor and
gouache on paper; dated 1907; 9 3/4 x 13 3/4 inches. SOHS Collection #1983.5.6.

Left bottom: PLATE #57
"Marine, Monterey, California." A scene of a rocky coastline painted at the same location as the image above
demonstrates Dorland's maturity of technique and style over time. This seascape was probably created between
1912 and 1914 while Dorland was living in California. Watercolor on paper; signed "R. Dorland Robinson";
no date; 8 x 13 inches. SOHS Collection #1978.20.11.

Above: PLATE #58

Dorland achieved a subtle elegance with this painting by contrasting a highly textured impasto foreground against a starkly smooth winter sky. Oil on canvas; signed "R.D. Robinson";
dated 1916; 12 x 15 inches. SOHS Collection #2003.53.1.

Right: PLATE #59

"Old Stage Road." Dorland interpreted the road that ran in front of her home and out of town in this rendering of a country lane after a rain. Oil on canvas; signed "R.D. Robinson"; dated 1916;
16 x 9 3/4 inches. SOHS Collection #1978.20.5.

Above: PLATE #61
Peter Britt's lily pond was among the Southern Oregon landscapes that Dorland liked to paint.
Watercolor on paper; signed "Dorland Robinson"; no date; 13 x 16 3/4 inches.
SOHS Collection #B231.

Left: PLATE #60
Jackson Creek, Jacksonville, Oregon. Dr. Robinson gave this painting to Jacksonville Presbyterian Church
pastor Reverend S.H. Jones and his wife. They in turn passed it on to their friends Roy and Gertrude Martin.
Watercolor on paper; no date; 13 1/2 x 10 1/2 inches.
Dorothy E. Martin Collection.

Appendix One:
ADDITIONAL WORKS OF ART BY DORLAND ROBINSON

Portraits

Nydah Neil, Jacksonville resident; friend of Dorland's (PLATE #66). Charcoal on light blue paper; signed "Regina Dorland Robinson"; dated 1909; 22 1/2 x 16 1/2 inches. SOHS Collection #1977.35.6.

Aderal Elmer (Hudson), Jacksonville resident; young girl seated at a table reading a magazine (PLATE #64). Sepia pressed pigment crayon on paper; signed "Regina Dorland Robinson"; dated 1909; 18 1/2 x 23 3/4 inches. SOHS Collection #1960.27.5.

Elizabeth T'Vault (Kenny), Jacksonville resident; elderly woman wearing a shawl, seated, reading a book. Charcoal on paper; signed with a smudged and unreadable signature; no date; 22 x 14 inches. SOHS Collection #4291.

PLATE #62

Portrait of a little boy, possibly a Jacksonville resident; seated on a hassock, wearing overalls and hat (PLATE #62). Charcoal on light blue paper; signed twice, "Dorland Robinson" with pencil and "Dorland Robinson 1908" with white crayon; dated 1908; 23 x 17 3/4 inches. SOHS Collection #1978.20.18.

Bust of man wearing a suit and tie, possibly a Jacksonville resident (PLATE #63). Charcoal on light blue paper; signed "R.D. Robinson"; dated 1908; 23 x 17 1/4. SOHS Collection #1978.20.20.

Young woman with head tilted, arm bent, and hand to head; possibly a Jacksonville resident (PLATE #68). Sepia pressed pigment crayon on paper; signed "Regina Dorland Robinson"; dated 1908; 15 x 11 1/2 inches; SOHS Collection #1979.26.6.

PLATE #63

Bust of a woman wearing a white blouse. Charcoal on paper; no date; 23 1/2 x 17 1/2 inches; SOHS Collection #1978.20.17.

Elderly woman wearing a white ascot, seated and reading a book. Charcoal on paper; signed twice, "Dorland Robinson" with charcoal and "Dorland Robinson" with pencil; dated 1908; 23 1/2 x 17 3/4 inches. SOHS Collection #1978.20.16.

Bust of an elderly woman wearing a headscarf. Charcoal on paper; signed "R.D. Robinson"; no date; 22 x 15 3/4 inches. SOHS Collection #1978.20.19.

Woman standing, wearing a sunbonnet. Charcoal on paper; signed "Dorland Robinson"; no date; 23 x 16 3/4 inches. SOHS Collection #1978.20.22.

PLATE #64

Full-length side view of an elderly woman wearing a white apron, seated in chair doing needlework. Presumed to be a class study done at the Oregon School of Art in Portland. Charcoal on paper; signed "R.D. Robinson"; date may be obscured by mat; 23 1/2 x 17 1/2 inches. SOHS Collection #1978.20.23.

Young woman, seated, wearing a classical drape (PLATE #65). Presumed to be a class study done at the Oregon School of Art in Portland. Charcoal on paper; no date; 23 3/4 x 18 inches. SOHS Collection #1979.26.4.

PLATE #65

Elderly man with beard, seated on a box in front of an open window. Oil on canvas; no date; 17 3/4 x 13 3/4 inches. SOHS Collection #1979.3.50.

Portrait of John Miller as a little boy, seated holding a ball. Subject was Dorland Robinson's younger cousin, son of John and Mabel Prim Miller. Oil on canvas; signed "Dorland Robinson"; no date; 21 x 15 inches. Private collection.

Bernice Myer (Hicks), Ashland resident, profile of little girl wearing a kimono and holding a fan. Watercolor and gouache; signed "Regina Dorland Robinson"; dated 1907. Private collection.

Bust of bearded man (PLATE #67). Oil on canvas; signed "R.D. Robinson"; no date; 21 x 16 1/2 inches; James Harbison, Jason Volkert Collection.

Carol Francis Neil (Vawter), Jacksonville resident; little girl wearing a blue dress and large blue and white bonnet. According to Francis Neil Vawter, the painting was done in the Britt studio. Oil on canvas; signed "Regina Dorland Robinson"; dated 1907; 15 3/4 x 13 1/2 inches. Neil, Florey, and Vawter Collection.

PLATE #66

Anna Kasshafer (Rumley), Jacksonville resident. During a 1977 interview, the subject mentioned Dorland did her portrait when she was a girl. Location unknown.

Ruthetta Ennis, Jacksonville resident; young girl sitting on a tree limb at the Britt grounds near the water ditch. Subject was the Presbyterian minister's daughter. In a 1980 interview, Mabel Reeve (Vroman) recalled being with Dorland and Ruthetta when the portrait was done. Location unknown.

Governor George Chamberlain. Subject was Oregon governor between 1903 and 1909. A portrait was sketched while Chamberlain made a July 4th speech and later completed with color and sent to the Governor; dated 1907; location unknown.

PLATE #67

George H. Williams, former Oregon Territory Chief Justice, U.S. Attorney General, and Portland Mayor. Oil on canvas; 1907. A likeness of this painting was published in the December 22, 1907 *Oregon Sunday Journal.* Location unknown.

John Sharp Williams, U.S. House of Representatives Minority Leader; probably a pencil sketch; 1908. Subject was drawn while he delivered a speech at the Ashland, Oregon Chautauqua. Location unknown.

U.S. President William Taft; probably a pencil sketch; ca. 1912. Presumably, Dorland saw the President when he was campaigning on the West Coast for his second term. She sent him the sketch and, according to the August 27, 1916 *Oregonian,* Taft returned a "cordial letter of endorsement." Location unknown.

Geraldine Gardner (Rode), Jacksonville resident. Subject was the daughter of Jackson County Clerk George A. Gardner and Clara Richardson Gardner. The

PLATE #68

painting was exhibited at the Holland Hotel, Medford, Oregon, January 21, 1916. Location unknown.

Delvan Smith, possibly an Ashland resident. Subject was the son of Professor F.C. Smith. The painting was exhibited at the Holland Hotel, Medford, Oregon, January 21, 1916. Location unknown.

Stella Johnson, brunette woman wearing a blue Mandarin robe, sitting in a wicker chair with a red lantern in the background. Exhibited at the Hotel Portland, August 1916 and Crawford's Art Shop in Burlingame, California; March 1917. Pastel; 1916; life-size; Location unknown.

Genevieve Holmberg Lyon, exhibited at the San Mateo High School, San Mateo, California, March 1917. Pastel; 1917; life-size; Location unknown

PLATE #69

Still Life Arrangements

Three blue thistles in a green vase (PLATE #69). Watercolor on paper; signed "R.D. Robinson"; dated 1913; 19 x 14 3/4 inches; SOHS Collection #1962.136.

Bunches of light and dark grapes on one side, (PLATE #70). California poppies in a glass jar on reverse side of the painting. Watercolor on paper; signed "R. Dorland Robinson"; no date; 10 x 17 inches. SOHS Collection #1978.20.24.

Glass bottle and brass pitcher on folded paper. Oil on canvas; no date; 23 3/4 x 17 1/2 inches. SOHS Collection #1979.26.2.

Light-colored painted china set with lid off the sugar bowl and a spoon and cherries in the foreground (PLATE #71). Oil on canvas, signed "Regina Dorland Robinson"; no date; 16 x 21 inches. SOHS Collection #1979.26.1.

PLATE #70

Dark ceramic teapot, white sugar bowl, and a ladle on a tray with a cup and saucer to the right on a highly polished table. Oil on canvas; 23 1/2 x 27 1/2 inches.; SOHS Collection #1978.20.29.

Fruit in a metal bowl with an oval portrait hanging on the wallpapered background. Oil on canvas; signed "Regina Dorland Robinson"; no date; 20 x 15 3/4 inches. SOHS Collection #1979.26.8.

Brass and copper pots with a blue and white teapot. One of several paintings given to Alice Becroft Mitchell by Dorland or her parents. Oil on canvas; no date; 21 1/4 x 19 1/4 inches. SOHS Collection #2004.123.

PLATE #71

Peaches in a silver bowl with sliced peach on a plate in the foreground. Watercolor on paper; signed "Regina Dorland Robinson"; dated 1911; 19 x 14 inches; Gary and Denece Zavoral Collection.

Bouquet of pink roses in blue vase (PLATE #72). May be one of five rose paintings exhibited at the Holland Hotel, Medford, Oregon, January 21, 1916. Oil on canvas; signed "Regina Dorland Robinson"; dated 1912; 32 x 23 inches. Flinn Family Collection.

Flared brass vase next to a clear glass globe in foreground, brown bowl or basket tilted up in the background. Oil on canvas; signed "Regina Dorland Robinson"; no date; 24 x 20 inches. Flinn Family Collection.

Two clear glasses, black bowl on white cloth in foreground with blue & white stoneware, black tea pot, and upturned bowl in back. Oil on canvas; no date; 18 x 24 inches. Perry Family Collection.

Three radishes in a stemmed glass, one radish on the table at the base of the glass. One of several paintings given to Alice Becroft Mitchell by Dorland or her parents. Oil on canvas; signed "Regina Dorland Robinson"; dated 1908; 11 1/2 x 8 inches. Elias Collection.

Brass pitcher laying on its side next to a standing copper urn with a blue drape in the background (PLATE #73). One of three paintings Dr. Robinson gave to his friend and physician, Dr. James C. Hayes, in the 1930s. Oil on canvas; signed "Dorland Robinson; no date; 23 1/2 x 19 1/2 inches. Private collection.

"After the Opera." Oil painting included as one of five paintings shown at the Annual Spring Exhibition of the San Francisco Art Association, 1912. No description given. Location unknown.

Interiors

Woman sitting in a pink bedroom (PLATE #74); Oil on canvas; signed "Dorland Robinson"; no date; 19 3/4 x 16 inches. SOHS Collection #1978.20.8.

"Morning Through a Window." Sunshine streaming through a window onto unknown subject. Described in the May 4, 1912, *Oakland Tribune*. Purchased in 1912 by Wickham Havens of Oakland, California. Location unknown.

Landscapes, Animals, and Buildings

Golden grass in foreground with water to the left, dark rolling hills and sky with clouds in the background. Watercolor on paper; signed "Regina Dorland Robinson"; no date; 5 1/4 x 8 1/2 inches. SOHS Collection #1983.5.4.

Green and golden grass in foreground with water to the left, green grass, rolling gray hills and sky with clouds in the background. Watercolor on paper; no date; 5 x 8 1/2 inches. SOHS Collection #1983.5.5.

Pasture scene with two reddish-brown cows in foreground, predominant colors are pastel pinks and blues. Oil on composition board; signed "Regina Dorland Robinson"; no date; 17 3/4 x 11 3/4 inches. SOHS Collection #1978.20.2.

"Foggy Day." Cluster of barns in a misty atmosphere painted in beige colors (PLATE #75). May have been exhibited at the Holland Hotel, Medford, Oregon, January 21, 1916. Oil on canvas, signed "Regina Dorland Robinson"; dated 1911; 10 1/4 x 14 inches. SOHS Collection #1978.20.3.

PLATE #72

PLATE #73

PLATE #74

PLATE #75

PLATE #76

PLATE #77

PLATE #78

"Old Tom." White horse with blurred contours stands in a stable or barn; Oil on composition board; signed "Regina Dorland Robinson"; unreadable date; 10 3/4x 13 1/2 inches; SOHS Collection #1978.20.7.

Stumps in a cleared field with log cabin to the left and a row of trees behind. Attributed to Dorland but may have been done by her father or someone else; primitive execution. This painting came from the Peter Britt estate. It was painted from a Britt photograph (SOHS Photo #7012) of the Granville Sears cabin. Oil on canvas; signed "R"; no date; 7 3/4 x 9 3/4inches. SOHS Collection #B355.

Carmel Mission, Carmel, California. (PLATE #76). Watercolor on paper; signed "Regina Dorland Robinson"; no date; 12 x 16 inches. Perry Family Collection.

"A Foggy Day." Tall trees on sandy ground surrounded by mist. The title, "A Foggy Day," is painted to the right of the signature (PLATE #77). This is likely the watercolor listed as "Foggy Day, Monterey, Cal." that was loaned by Mrs. John Opp for the exhibition at the Holland Hotel, Medford, Oregon, January 21, 1916. Watercolor on paper; signed "Regina Dorland Robinson." Private collection.

Rural landscape with stream in the foreground. Gouache on paper; signed "Regina Dorland Robinson"; dated 1909; 12 x 16 inches; Perry Family Collection.

Rural landscape in fall colors. Gouache on paper; signed "Regina Dorland Robinson"; dated 1908; 12 x 16 inches. Perry Family Collection.

Little bird sketch. Pencil on paper; measurements unknown. Private collection.

Seascapes

Two-masted sailing ship anchored in a bay with a small rowboat in foreground and a sailboat in background. Watercolor on paper; signed "Dorland Robinson"; no date; 11 1/2 x 9° inches. SOHS Collection #1957.93.2.

Large rocks with calm ocean beyond. Watercolor on paper; signed "R. Dorland"; 9 3/4 x 13 inches. SOHS Collection #60.94.

Portfolio of Eighth Grade School Work (includes following drawings)

Yellow irises with ship in cameo at the center (PLATE #78). Signed "Dorland Robinson"; watercolor on paper.

Four illustrated essays: "The Mistletoe," pen and ink drawing of a tree; "Tempo," pen and ink drawing of a metronome; "Labor and Fish Problems," pen and ink drawing of a fish; "The Skeleton," pen and ink drawing of a skeleton (PLATES #79, #80).

Drawing of a Dutch-style windmill with a cemetery in the foreground. Pencil on paper; signed "Dorland Robinson Eight Grade."

Two black ink silhouettes. One of a woman sitting on a stool and one of a pitcher. Both are signed "Dorland Robinson Eight Grade."

Portfolio of Unframed Contour Drawings and Informal Sketches in the SOHS Collection

Nine contour drawings of classical figures that may have been drawn from plaster statues as class assignments either at the Oregon School of Art, or at the Pennsylvania Academy of the Fine Arts. Pencil on tracing paper. SOHS Collection #1979.3.52 through #1979.3.67

Sixteen quick sketches of men, women, and children in various poses. Pencil on paper; some are signed (PLATES #81, #82 and #83). SOHS Collection #1979.3.52 through #1979.3.67

PLATE #79

PLATE #81

PLATE #82

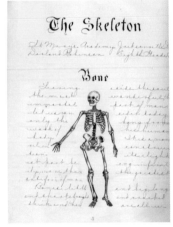

PLATE #80

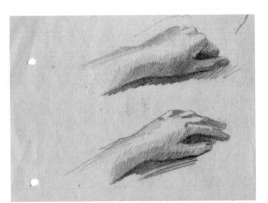

PLATE #83

Appendix Two:
LETTERS BY REGINA DORLAND ROBINSON

While growing up in Jacksonville, Oregon, Dorland Robinson became acquainted with three sisters, Mildred Neil (Florey), Nydah Neil, and Carol Frances Neil (Vawter). Below are typed transcripts of five hand written letters Dorland wrote to two of these young women. Four of the letters were written in 1912 and 1913 to Mildred who was two years older than Dorland. One is to Frances, the youngest sister who was sixteen years old in 1916, the year it is believed that the undated letter was written. Letters courtesy of Carroll Bacigalupi.

Letter dated July 22, 1912
Envelope address to Miss Mildred Niel [sic],
Jacksonville, Oregon
c/o Judge J. Niel [sic]
[Oakland, California postmark, Panama-Pacific Exposition stamp cancellation]

July 22-12

Dear Mildred
　　I certainly feel like a heathen or a Hottentot not to have answered your kind letter before, but the days slip by like — sand through my fingers; also my scanty literary powers have been about exhausted writing letters to papa. Mama or I write one every day, only think of it! while he,—poor man, writes as many as we.

　　In your letter you were inquiring about the weather, were you not? Not being a weather bureau, however, I dont know that I can make out a very creditable report. We have had almost no fog as yet, and such as there was, (it was quite high), melted away in the afternoon, when the sun shone again. There were three days in June of very warm weather, when the attic was a small but a wonderfully life-like edition of the "Lower Regions," – when in a spirit of desperation we "hied" our selves to town and bought a refrigerator, also some thin underwear. But directly, it became quite cool again, so we had not, then, very much use for either. Just now it is delightful, quite warm in the middle of the day while the mornings and evenings are cool.

　　Since you were here I think five houses have been completed on our street together with the one back of it. How did all the photographs that you "took" down here develope [sic]?, Mildred, write and tell me, won't you? and all that you & Nydah are doing, too,—I most truly will answer sooner, another time; — with our kindest regards for Mr & Mrs. Niel [sic], Nydah, Frances, & yourself, I am

Sincerely your friend
Dorland Robinson

Letter dated December 7, 1912
Envelope address to Miss Mildred Niel [sic],
Derby via Eagle Point, Oregon.
c/o Mr Frank R. Niel [sic]
[Oakland, California postmark, Panama-Pacific Exposition stamp cancellation]

Dear Mildred,

I received the letter and the photographs from you, such a long time ago; and here am I, again 'steen weeks after date, with nothing in the world to plead but "guilty"! And I may not do even that with dignity, for after all my protestations it is really too, — funny. I think the mental wireless you suggested would be splendid.

The post-cards are beautiful, in some parts they have those qualities one finds in paintings. I liked especially that of the Japanese garden in the Park, & the one you took when we were together on Knob Hill.

By the way, I wish we could be together again this winter on Knob Hill—(or otherwise,) or that you were all coming down — wouldn't [it] be delightful, at least I think it would be.

The weather is beautiful now, although we had a great deal of rain the first part of last month, rain that converted the back-yard into one vast puddle, where my six cats, (you didn't know I had six cats) paddled around, and no doubt lost their tempers over it. If you were only a bit more interested in them, (the cats) I might even go into details, but there, — there, I won't do it.

We have not gone up to Tamalpias [sic] yet , but Mama and I go around so little alone, Papa not being with us. However he is coming down soon and I shall let you guess, (amazing riddle) exactly how happy we will be then!

Grandma was with us Thanksgiving week, and she told me that you were at home now. So I am addressing this most woefully belated letter to you there.

Good-by then, "Fraulein," "Wollen Sie mir nicht wieder schreiben?" but there I "go" again! it must be either pussycats or Dutch, felines or Frauleins!

With our kindest regards for Mr. and Mrs Niel [sic], Nydah, Frances, and yourself, I am with love

> *Ever Dorland*
> *Oakland,*
> *Dec 7, 1912*

Letter dated December 31, 1912
Envelope addressed to Miss Mildred Niel [sic]
Derby via Eagle Point, Oregon.
[Oakland, California postmark, Panama Pacific Exposition stamp cancellation]
"Prospect" is written in another hand on the envelope.

Dear Mildred

Received the photographs safely; such a pleasant surprise; Thank you so much for them.

I certainly do like sheep and these are so lovely—as lovely as any sheep photograph I have ever seen, even down to that most delightful bit of water in the "foreground" with the tree reflections falling into it.

As for the other,—really you are entirely too modest, for you never told me you had such a splendid place, but I looked in vain for at least one of you on the long porch and could not find even Frances bright head popping up among the planks.

We had such a lovely Christmas here, the sky was so blue, and the sunshine so bright, but it was cold—real Christmas cold.

Good-by now—"Fraulein." Write to me when you can spare the time will you not.

With our kindest regards and Good Wishes for the New Year's Happiness of all our friends at the "Pines", I am, with love,

> *Dorland*
> *Dec 31 – 1912*
> *Oakland, California.*

Letter dated August 12, 1913
Envelope address to Miss Mildred Niel [sic]
Derby, Oregon
[Jacksonville, Oregon postmark]

Dear Mildred

Its such a terribly long time since I received your letter that I am probably headed straight for the place, (supposing there is one) reserved for those wretched people who don't answer the letters other people are good enough to write to them.

But perhaps you know that Papa has been very very sick, and have been kind enough to make some allowances.

So sorry I did not see you and Nydah when you were over, but really I did not know you were here at all till some time after when the Judge told me you had gone. But you will be here again, wont you?

The weather is really delightful now

In your letter that I received so long ago that I am quite hazy about it, you asked me about a certain book on photography that I had spoken of, did you not? Now before I came up, I went over the books on photography at the Oakland Library, read a few of them, but could not find the one I spoke of, or any other especially practical.

The one I refered [sic] to (I read it in the East) was either by Clarence White or Gertrude Kassibier [Kasebier], both leading New York photographers, but the title I have forgotten. It was really a very good book.

Goodby now Fraulein, forgive if you can this latest offence against the laws of letterwriting Hoping to see you and Nydah and the "kleine" (?) sister soon and with best love to you all I am

Dorland
Tuesday
August 12, 1913

Dorland wrote to Frances following a visit she had recently made to the Neil family ranch, known as "The Pines," near Butte Falls, Oregon.

Undated letter
Envelope addressed to Miss Francis Niel [sic]
Prospect, Oregon via Pacific & Eastern
[Jacksonville, Oregon postmark]
Back of envelope has notation saying "summer 1916"

Wednesday
My dear Francis:

Am safely landed at home, after a very pleasant week, spent with a most delightful family, one mile and one half from Derby Station!

The week has many a pleasant recollection of schottish [sic] and three-step, ice-tea and pink sherbet, a picnic and a fishing-trip, chocolate cake and taffy—and, just lots of things.

So sorry, but was unable to locate the "Ouija" board, for you, in Medford. I tried the "Wonder Store" "Book Store" & "Ten Cent Store" However the first has some ordered, so told them to reserve one for you, and I shall send it out to you as soon as possible.

Am also mailing you some pink poplin and dotted – swiss for the top of my dressing table. I was so very unfortunate as to upset on it some of that nice rich milk, given me to drink—didn't discover it till it had been there all day, by which time it was pretty well soaked in. Am so very sorry.

Thanking you all for a lovely week, and with kindest regards from the family. I am

Sincerely
Dorland R

Do hope Mildred's poison oak is better now.

Appendix Three:
EXHIBITION LIST

Annual Spring Exhibition of the San Francisco Art Association
Held at the San Francisco Institute of Art, San Francisco, California, April 5 through May 3, 1912

1. *Sunlight, Rogue River Valley* (oil)
2. *After the Opera*, still life (oil)
3. *Misty Day* (oil)
4. *Nasturtiums* (watercolor)
5. *Yellow Roses* (watercolor)

[A May 4, *Oakland Tribune* article about this exhibit referred to two paintings by name. One, *Misty Morning in Rogue River Valley* was probably, *Sunlight, Rogue River Valley*. The other, *Morning Through a Window* does not correlate with the catalog list above.

Annual Spring Exhibition of the San Francisco Art Association
Held at the San Francisco Institute of Art, San Francisco, California, April 4 through May 3, 1913

1. Still life (oil)
2. *Reflections* (oil)

Exhibition of Paintings of Regina Dorland Robinson
January 21, 1916, Holland Hotel, Medford, Oregon

1. *Two Roses*
2. *Autumn Afternoon* [sold]
3. *Sunlight, Rogue River Valley* (oil)
4. *Almond Blossoms* (oil)
5. *A Spring Morning*
6. *Peach Blossoms* (oil)
7. *Foggy Day* (oil)
8. *Poplars in Autumn*
9. *First Snow*, 1916 (oil)

10. *Foggy Morning* (oil)
11. *A Wintry Day*, 1916 (oil)
12. *Roxy Ann*
13. *La France Roses*
14. *Roses*
15. *Full-Blown Roses* (Loaned by Judge F. TouVelle)
16. *A Salad* (watercolor)
17. *Peaches* (opaque watercolor and pastel)
18. *Blue and Gold*
19. *Yellow Roses* (watercolor)
20. *Nasturtiums* (watercolor and pastel)
21. *Dahlias*
22. *Chinatown*, Monterey, Cal.
23. *Foggy Day*, Monterey, Cal. (watercolor) (Loaned by Mrs. John Opp)
24. *Sand Dunes and Cypress*
25. Portrait Geraldine Gardner (Loaned by Mrs. George Gardner)
26. Portrait Delevan Smith (Loaned by Professor F.C. Smith)
27. Still Life
28. Still Life
29. *Dahlias*
30. *Afternoon Tea*
31. *The Back Door*
32. *The Fish Bowl*
33. *The China Lily*
34. *Five o'Clock Tea*
35. Portrait Study

Hotel Portland, Portland, Oregon
August 1916

1. Life-sized portrait of Stella Johnson (pastel)

Fifth Annual Exhibition of the Works of Artists of the Pacific Northwest
Portland Art Association, Portland, Oregon, November 14–December 10, 1916

1. *Misty Morning* (oil)
2. *May Day* (oil)
3. *Cactus Dahlias* (oil)
4. *Winter 1916* (oil)
5. *First Snow* (oil)
6. Portrait Miss Mildred Neil (pastel) (Lent by Miss Neil)

Crawford Art Shop, *Burlingame, California, March 1917*

1. Life-sized portrait of Stella Johnson (pastel)
2. Self-portrait (pastel)

San Mateo High School, *San Mateo, California March 9, 1917*

1. Life-sized portrait of Genevieve Holmberg Lyon (pastel)

ENDNOTES

1. As late as 2006, an owner of a Dorland Robinson painting mentioned the bigamy theory in conversation. A number of Oral History (OH) transcripts in the Southern Oregon Historical Society (SOHS) archives, including OH 160, p.14; OH 166, p.13; OH 221,p. 31; and OH 258, p.3, allude to other unsubstantiated theories mentioned in this text.

2. Photographs in the SOHS archives show Dr. and Mrs. Robinson with Emil and Molly Britt taken in 1918 and 1924. A number of works of art by Dorland Robinson now in the SOHS collection came from the Britt estate. For more about Peter Britt and the German community in Jacksonville, see "Man of Culture, Man of Commerce: Peter Britt 1819-1905" by Dawna Curler. *Southern Oregon Heritage Today*, Summer 2004, Vol.6 No. 4.

3. The lives of Dr. Robinson and Tillie Miller are summarized in two articles by Ray Lewis published by the SOHS: "Frontier Physician Takes Active Part in Community," *The Table Rock Sentinel*, March 1981, and "Tillie," *The Table Rock Sentinel*, February 1985.

4. Robinson family scrapbook, MS 60, SOHS.

5. There is confusion over Dorland's birth date. Some secondary sources say 1892 because that is the date erroneously carved on Dorland's gave marker. A birth announcement in the *Democratic Times*, November 6, 1891 and other primary sources document November 5, 1891 as her true date of birth.

6. Citations in the *Democratic Times* between November 13, 1891 and May 6, 1892 chronicled construction of the house. Like the Nunan House next door, the Robinson House was built from plans ordered through architect George F. Barber's catalog, *The Cottage Souvenir*. The 1892 edition shows the floor plan used by the Robinsons and includes a testimonial letter from H.F. Wood, the contractor who built the house. In his letter he states, "I have just completed the residence for Dr. J.W. Robinson.... The house is a gem and we are pleased with it, as are, also, the neighbors. I have, through it, obtained the contract for J. Newman's [a misspelling of Nunan] house, to be built from plans furnished by you. I recommend your book of designs to those who wish beautiful homes."

7. Don J. Russell, interviewed April 11, 1984. SOHS OH 303, p.7. Jeremiah Nunan was the Robinson's next-door neighbor. Don Russell was Nunan's grandson.

8. Mabel A. Reeve Vroman, interviewed June 18, 1980. SOHS OH 159 pps. 5, 7, 9.

9. Albert Augustine Mitchell, interviewed August 12, 1980. SOHS OH 166, p.11.

10. Anna Caroline Niedermeyer Wendt, interviewed June 19, 1980. SOHS OH 160, p.11.

11. Russell, OH 303, p.7 and Wendt, OH 160, p. 12.

12. Notes from a conversation with Louise Williamson Issacs, undated, presumably taken by Ray Lewis. Robinson Vertical File, SOHS.

13. Anna Kasshafer Rumley, interviewed March 24, 1977. SOHS OH 85, p.12.

14. 1900 Federal census for Jackson County.

15. Letter from Dorland Robinson to Mildred Neil, July 22, 1912, Oakland, CA; letter from Dorland Robinson to Mildred Neil, December 9, 1912, Oakland, CA; letter from Dorland Robinson to Mildred Neil, December 31, 1912, Oakland, CA; letter from Dorland Robinson to Mildred Neil, August 12, 1913, Jacksonville, OR; letter from Dorland Robinson to Francis Neil, Jacksonville, OR, summer 1916. Carroll Bacigalupi family papers. The author of the photography book Dorland mentions was either Clarence White or Gertrude Kassibier, Dorland could not remember which.

16. Chronicles, St. Mary's Academy, Jacksonville, OR, June 13, 1904; June 15, 1904; and June 16, 1905. Sisters of the Holy Names of Jesus and Mary, Archives, Portland, OR; *Medford Mail Tribune*, December 27, 1908.

17. *Medford Mail Tribune*, April 24, 1915. The card game 500 was fashionable in the early 20th century and "500 Clubs" were popular throughout the nation.

18. JoAnne Mitchell Elias. Handwritten note, SOHS collections records.

19. Mitchell, OH 166, p. 9. In slight variance to Albert Mitchell's statement that Dorland gave the paintings to Alice, his daughter, JoAnne Elias thought the artwork was given to Alice and Albert by Mr. and Mrs. Robinson after Dorland's death. Three sketches by Alice Becroft (Mitchell) are in the SOHS collection. These and more of Becroft's work privately owned, are published in "The Sketchbook of Alice Becroft," by Mary Ames Sheret; *Southern Oregon Heritage*, Vol. 3, No. 3, 1998.

20. Although the Medford section of the 1916 Jackson County Directory lists Johnson as an agent for the Pacific and Eastern Railroad, May 1 and September 29, 1915, *Medford Mail Tribune* citations refers to him as "superintendent."

21. *Medford Mail Tribune*, November 18, 1916.

22. Stella Johnson is not mentioned in newspaper articles reviewing the January 1916 exhibit of Dorland Robinson artwork at the Holland Hotel in Medford; however, an April 7, 1917 *Medford Mail Tribune* article indicates Mrs. Geo. Johnson was on the committee for "hanging and lighting of pictures" for a second exhibition planned that month. In a 1992 letter written to Sue Waldron from Carrol Bacigalupi, daughter of Carol Frances Neil Vawter, the youngest Neil sister, Bacigalupi stated that her 92-year-old mother said the Neil girls rented rooms from Stella Johnson during part of 1915 and 1916.

23. *Medford Sun*, May 20, 1917; obituary for John Shaule, *Oregon Journal*, September 26, 1917; Federal Census 1900-1930; grave registry, Riverview Cemetery, Portland; Denver City Directories, Colorado Historical Society; and personal correspondence between Shaule family descendents and Sue Waldron begun in September 2005.

24. *Medford Mail Tribune*, October 30, 1916.

25. The 1916 San Francisco city directory lists Charles Henry Pearson as the manager for Yale-Towne Manufacturing Co. and residing at 308 Eddy St. There is no mention of Pearson in the 1915 city directory, which may indicate he was not in the city when Dorland and her parents first visited the Exposition.

26. "Artist's Return From Art Exhibit," *Medford Mail Tribune*, May 8, 1916.

27. *Medford Mail Tribune*, December 14, 1916.

28. *Jacksonville Post*, January 6, 1917.

29. Photocopies of Dorland Robinson's marriage registration, interlocutory divorce decree, and death certificate, Dorland Robinson Vertical file, SOHS.

30. Military record for Charles Henry Pearson issued by the War Department. Form No.84c-1, A.G.O., October 18, 1922, New York State Archives, Albany. It is interesting to note that Dorland took her life on April 7, 1917, the day after the United States entered World War I.

31. Information about Charles Henry Pearson was reconstructed from the following sources: Federal Census for 1900-1930; Social Security record, Form SS-5; *New York Times* obituary, November 16, 1968; Death Certificate issued by the City of New York, Department of Health, Office of Vital Records; San Francisco City Directories, 1914-1917, California Historical Society; New York City Directories, New York City Historical Society; Portland City Directory, 1917, Oregon Historical Society; Spokane City Directories 1943-1956, public library, Spokane, Washington; grave registry, Green-Wood Cemetery, Brooklyn, New York.

32. Dorland Robinson Vertical File, SOHS.

33. "Miss Robinson A Suicide," *Medford Sun*, April 8, 1917. Copy in Robinson Vertical File, SOHS.

34. Dorland's artwork was discovered in 1978. Now part of the SOHS's collection, they were found in a file drawer in a room that had once been a St. Mary's Academy office. In 1905, the year these works were created, schools throughout the St. Mary's Academy system collected student work to show at the Lewis and Clark Centennial Exhibition in Portland. Although further research is needed, it is speculated that these works, or some like them, may have been created for that purpose.

35. *Medford Mail*, November 9, 1906 and *Medford Mail*, March 8, 1907.

36. Most known examples of Dorland's 1907 portraits of children were painted with watercolor and gouache; however, she did a remarkably well executed oil dated 1907 of seven-year-old Carol Frances Neil. This painting is presumed to have been done prior to the Portland art lessons.

37. *Oregon Journal*, August 25, 1907. The Metschans were in-laws of Tillie's sister, Mollie. Phil Metschan owned the Imperial Hotel, which is where the Robinsons stayed for a number of months when they took Dorland to Portland for art lessons.

38. *Jacksonville Post*, September 21, 1907. Dorland made sketches of other dignitaries. She had a similar response from President Taft whom she probably saw in 1912 when he was campaigning on the West coast for a second term. The August 27, 1916 *Oregonian* stated, "Ex-President Taft was so delighted with a little sketch of himself that he sent Miss Robinson a cordial letter of endorsement."

39. *Oregon Sunday Journal*, December 22, 1907. This article states an oil painting of Judge George Williams by Dorland Robinson was displayed at the Oregon School of Art in the Selling-Hirsch building and identifies Miss Florence Chase Currier, from Boston, as the director of the school. The 1907-1908 Portland city directory lists Currier as the director of the Oregon School of Art, rooms 72-76, in the Selling-Hirsch building at 386 ½ Washington St. The 1909 and 1910 city directories show the Oregon School of Art located in the Oregon Building at the Lewis and Clark Fairgrounds. The 1910 directory lists Currier as the director. No listing for the school or Currier appears in the 1911 directory; however, Currier did exhibit at the 1912 regional exhibition at the Portland Art Museum.

40. *Oregon Sunday Journal*, December 22, 1907. Although this article only refers to Williams as Judge, earlier in his career he was an Oregon Territory Chief Justice, U.S. Senator, and U.S. Attorney General. He served as Portland mayor from 1902 to 1905 and died in 1910.

41. "Girl Artist Found." *Oregonian*, August 27, 1916. This article about Dorland and the portrait of Stella Johnson exhibited at the Portland Hotel states, "Colonel C.E.S. Wood has some of her pictures and admires them greatly."

42. *The Spectator*, February 26, 1910 and "Burlingame Home of Talented Artist," *San Mateo County News*, March 8, 1917.

43. Mabel Reeve Vroman, interviewed June 18, 1980, OH 159, p. 6. Albert Mitchell also mentioned this tree near the Britt ditch during his 1980 interview. He said it was a laurel tree and was "a place where they used to go and sit and make love." Mitchel, OH 166, pp. 12-13.

44. Molly Walker Kerr. "Chautauqua: The Cultural Spark that Ignited Ashland," *Table Rock Sentinel*, Summer, 1992.

45. Frances Bernice Myer Hicks, interviewed July 30, 1982. SOHS OH, 258, p.3.

46. *Medford Daily Tribune*, July 14, 1908.

47. *Jacksonville Post*, September 24, 1910 and May 6, 1911.

48. Various newspaper articles suggest that Dorland took training from Henry Rittenberg or William Merritt Chase. Chase did teach at PAFA, but not when Dorland attended. Rittenberg attended PAFA as a student and was a board member in the Academy Fellowship (alumni club) when Dorland was there, but he was never on the faculty. No documentation has been found showing Dorland studied with either artist. Letters from Cheryl Leibold, Archivist, Pennsylvania Academy of the Fine Arts to Sue Waldron: January 16, 2006, April 7, 2004, and April 14, 1992.

49. Founded in 1887 by nine women artists who had studied at the California School of Design, the Sketch Club was originally a women's sketch group. By 1909, it included men. *The Oakland Tribune*, April 10, 1909 lists Arthur and Lucia Mathews, Martinez, and Bremer as members exhibiting in a Sketch Club exhibition. Lucia Mathews was president that year and Bremer was on the board of directors. Sargeant was a co-founder and longtime member of the Sketch Club. In 1914 the group changed its name to the San Francisco Society of Artists. [*The Oakland Tribune*, October 14, 1914] Many Sketch Club members were also associated with the San Francisco

Art Association. Sargeant became the director of the San Francisco Art Association in 1915 when it merged with the San Francisco Society of Artists.

50. Ellen Halteman. "Exhibition Record of the San Francisco Art Association 1872-1915," Publications in *California Art* No. 7. Los Angeles: Dustin Publications, 2000, p. 260. According to this listing, the five paintings Dorland displayed were *Sunlight, Rogue River Valley* (oil); *After the Opera*, still life (oil); *Misty Day* (oil); *Nasturtiums* (watercolor); and *Yellow Roses* (watercolor).

51. *Oakland Tribune*, May 4, 1912. The other painting in this article was *Misty Morning in Rogue River Valley*, which probably referred to the painting in the SOHS collection, *Sunlight, Rogue River Valley* cited above. *Morning Through a Window* was purchased by Mr. Wickham Havens, the son of real-estate mogul Frank C. Havens. The article also claimed that the Robinsons had visited galleries in "the art centers of Europe" where Dorland "had the advantage of fine training." No mention of a trip abroad has been found in any other documentation; it is unlikely that they ever left the country.

52. Alice Brown Chittenden was an active Bay Area art teacher and wildflower, landscape, and portrait artist. She painted in oils and pastels. Chittenden studied and later taught at the California School of Design and also studied and exhibited in New York, France, and Italy. She was one of the first two women to exhibit at the previously all-male Bohemian Club exhibition in 1898 and one of the founders of the Sketch Club in San Francisco. She was one of the dominant women figures in the Bay Area art world.

53. Several of Dorland's obituaries mention that she showed artwork at the Panama-Pacific Exposition, which is doubtful. There are no such mentions of this fact before or after April 1917. Dorland was not listed among Oregon artists exhibiting at the exposition. A list of California artists has not yet been checked for her name.

54. *Medford Mail Tribune*, May 8, 1916.

55. Dorland Robinson vertical file, SOHS, contains a list of paintings shown at the January 21, 1916 exhibit, and several newspaper clippings describing the exhibit. A report in the *Medford Mail Tribune*, October 28, 1916 indicates Dorland was a member of the Greater Medford Club.

56. *The Oregonian*, August 27, 1916 and the *Portland Evening Telegram*, August 26, 1916. *The Oregonian* says "blue mandarin coat" and "rich red lantern," the *Evening Telegram* says, "kimono" and "a great Japanese lantern." A later description in the *San Mateo County News*, March 8, 1917, says "diaphanous Chinese mandarin robe" and "a huge lantern in the background."

57. *Oregonian*, November 19, 1916; Fifth Annual Exhibition of the Works of Artists of the Pacific Northwest, Portland Art Association, flyer published by the Museum of Art listing artist and artworks.

58. *San Mateo County News*, March 8, 1917. Contact with Dr. Offield's family revealed how he acquired the portrait.

59. *Medford Mail Tribune*, April 7, 1917.

60. Sue Waldron. "A Brief Bloom," *Table Rock Sentinel*, Summer, 1992, p.44.

The following individuals and organizations have graciously loaned and/or donated Dorland Robinson works to the Southern Oregon Historical Society's permanent collection:

Ackley, Maude A.
Bacigalupi, Carrol L
Ballard, Bess Kenney
Bernard, Virginia Bandy
Bowen, Marion
Carpenter, Alfred S.V.
Collins, Robertson
Elias, JoAnne
Hanley, E.B. Jr.
Heffernan, Kathryn
Heffernan, Mr. Robert
Hudson, Aderah Elmer
Jester, Jean W.
Johnson, Julia Opp
Matlack, Tresa
Mitchell, Alice Beacroft
Oregon State Board of Education
Snedecor, Jane
University of Oregon
Van Dyke, Gladys